T0361281

Cambridge Elements ≡

Elements in Religion and Monotheism
edited by
Paul K. Moser
Loyola University Chicago
Chad Meister
*Affiliate Scholar, Ansari Institute for Global Engagement with Religion,
University of Notre Dame*

MONOTHEISM AND NARRATIVE DEVELOPMENT OF THE DIVINE CHARACTER IN THE HEBREW BIBLE

Mark McEntire
Belmont University

CAMBRIDGE
UNIVERSITY PRESS

Shaftesbury Road, Cambridge CB2 8EA, United Kingdom

One Liberty Plaza, 20th Floor, New York, NY 10006, USA

477 Williamstown Road, Port Melbourne, VIC 3207, Australia

314–321, 3rd Floor, Plot 3, Splendor Forum, Jasola District Centre,
New Delhi – 110025, India

103 Penang Road, #05–06/07, Visioncrest Commercial, Singapore 238467

Cambridge University Press is part of Cambridge University Press & Assessment,
a department of the University of Cambridge.

We share the University's mission to contribute to society through the pursuit of
education, learning and research at the highest international levels of excellence.

www.cambridge.org
Information on this title: www.cambridge.org/9781009467841

DOI: 10.1017/9781009238984

First published 2023

A catalogue record for this publication is available from the British Library

ISBN 978-1-009-46784-1 Hardback
ISBN 978-1-009-23896-0 Paperback
ISSN 2631-3014 (online)
ISSN 2631-3006 (print)

Monotheism and Narrative Development of the Divine Character in the Hebrew Bible

Elements in Religion and Monotheism

DOI: 10.1017/9781009238984
First published online: December 2023

Mark McEntire
Belmont University

Author for correspondence: Mark McEntire, mark.mcentire@belmont.edu

Abstract: The preeminent example of monotheism, the God of the Hebrew Bible, is the end product of a long process. The world from which this literature emerged was polytheistic. The nature and arrangement of the literature diminishes polytheistic realities and enhances the effort to portray a single divine being. The development of this divine character through the course of a sustained narrative with a sequential plot aided the move toward monotheism by allowing for the placement of diverse, even conflicting, portrayals of the deity at distant points along the plot line. Through the sequence of events the divine character becomes more withdrawn from the sphere of human activity, more aged in appearance and behavior, and increasingly disembodied. All these characteristics lend themselves to the presentation of disparate narrative portrayals as a singular subject in this Element.

Keywords: Monotheism, character development, Hebrew Bible, ancient Israel, narrative

ISBNs: 9781009467841 (HB), 9781009238960 (PB), 9781009238984 (OC)
ISSNs: 2631-3014 (online), 2631-3006 (print)

Contents

1 Making a God in a Landscape of Gods

Monotheistic faith and the Hebrew Bible go hand in hand for most readers of the book that Judaism and Christianity hold sacred, but this is more of a perception of readers than a thorough depiction of the history of these traditions. By the time most of the Hebrew Bible was written, ancient Judaism had made moves toward monotheism, but this was a diverse milieu and ideas that did not fit neatly into a monotheistic framework were abundant. We might even presume this is why some biblical traditions have to argue so hard for monotheism.[1] They are having an argument with other traditions that differed. Likewise, throughout its history, Christianity has struggled to find ways to express its diverse understandings of Jesus Christ and the Holy Spirit that fit within a definition of monotheism. The monotheisms of Judaism and Christianity exist in great tension, were achieved from a background of diverse divine portrayals, and are continuously developing in a foreground of complex and expanding practices.

Whether monotheism is distinct to Judaism and the religious systems that developed in its wake, Christianity and Islam, depends upon the definition of monotheism. Gavin Flood has argued, for instance, that monotheism is a useful lens for examining aspects of Hinduism, a cultural-religious system most would readily identify as polytheistic. When Flood describes the monotheistic aspects of Hinduism, however, it likely sounds different to most readers from the monotheism that emerges from the Hebrew Bible and its successors.[2] For most Bible readers there is a single, united, consistent character called God, but this idea emerged from carefully crafted scribal practices and reading procedures. Flood's political analysis of the development of Hindu monotheism in the eighteenth and nineteenth centuries is particularly helpful, because it shows how these ideas can grow out of a response to colonial power. In contexts with large differentials of power, the survival of beliefs and ideas may require greater precision. The extent to which the colonized must adapt to the framework of the colonizer in order to be intelligible in that context stands in contrast to the desire to use the more traditional resources of the colonized culture in acts of resistance against imperialism.[3] The parallels to Judaism in the Persian and Hellenistic periods are not difficult to see. The same tension between accommodation and resistance was at play as the Jewish expression of its deity in the Hebrew Bible was arriving at the place now familiar to those who read these texts. The development of the books of the Bible and the forming of those books

---

[1] See the review of these traditions in Peter Schäfer, *Two Gods in Heaven: Jewish Concepts of God in Antiquity*, trans. Allison Brown (Princeton, NJ: Princeton University Press, 2020), 1–16.

[2] Gavin Flood, *Hindu Monotheism* (Cambridge: Cambridge University Press, 2020), 1–14.

[3] See the much more detailed discussion in ibid., 56–61.

into various collections was always an act of negotiation, both within communities and with the worlds around them. How to name and describe the divine character were among many ideas under negotiation and often served to connect many of the others.

Monotheism is sometimes portrayed as the end of an evolutionary development in belief about deities. Those portraying it this way are often related to monotheistic traditions, so such claims should be greeted with suspicion, as they portray a cultural supremacy over ways pejoratively labeled "pagan." The deity of the Bible, who is worshipped in Judaism, Christianity, and Islam is the model of a monotheistic deity, but it is important to ask how this figure came into that condition. Careful reading of transmitted texts, combined with the examination of material remains, reveals that the monotheism of these traditions was a hard-earned status. There was not a straight line of development, and there are no permanently fixed results. The long narrative of the Hebrew Bible, which Christianity adopted as the beginning of its own scriptures, and from which Islam took its list of prophets, makes monotheism possible despite the widely divergent depictions of deity it contains. As Daniel McClellan has explained in his novel exploration of the role cognition plays in the formulation of deities, "the emerging technology of text facilitated the cumulative and layered aggregation over time of these different approaches to deity, collapsing the disparities of time and space that had previously separated these ideas, thereby enriching and expanding the literary palette of those who would come after."[4] This approach also demonstrates how more generic conceptions of a deity become more complex and specific in response to a particular set of human experiences.

Monotheism as a belief that there is only one deity in the world required two distinct movements in ancient Israel. First, on a local level all the rival gods of YHWH had to be eliminated. Second, the understanding of YHWH needed to expand, so that YHWH could be the deity of all people in all places. The Hebrew Bible does not present a consistent picture of either of these processes, but there is a discernible sense of movement in these directions.

1.1 Gods in the Area

The closest deity to the God of the Bible in terms of chronology, geography, and character was Baal/Hadad, a being with origins in Mesopotamia who also found expression in Phoenicia and Canaan in the Late Bronze and Early Iron Ages. This deity known by the name Baal is the chief rival of YHWH in the Bible. The famous contest between Elijah (whose name means "my god is YHWH") and

---

[4] Daniel O. McClellan, *YHWH's Divine Images: A Cognitive Approach* (Atlanta, GA: SBL Press, 2022), 132–133.

the prophets of Baal on Mount Carmel in 1 Kings 18 may be the most familiar expression of this rivalry. The narrator of Kings blames the presence of Baal prophets in Israel on the Phoenician queen Jezebel, whom King Ahab had married. Worship of this deity is the reason for a drought YHWH uses to punish Israel, and Elijah emerges demanding Israel do what his own name declares.

While the Bible presents Baal in a negative light, as a rival god or a deity worshipped through images, there are important texts from the area that present him from the perspective of his own adherents. The famous Baal Cycle presents a series of events in the life of the deity, most famously Baal's defeat of the sea, the building of Baal's house, and Baal overcoming death.[5] These three tales seem to fall in a necessary sequence, but the series falls far short of the long and complex plot that presents the life of Israel's deity in the Hebrew Bible, and the events in the life of Baal are not connected to a series of human events taking place on earth. A good example of this difference is the movement of deities from their places of origin in mountainous abodes to the houses (temples) their subjects build for them in cities. Baal Sapan, a name connecting this deity to a mountain, finds his way to an urban temple, becoming Baal of Ugarit, but the former identity persists.[6] The deity has no problem being connected to two places. This duality might represent a problem for Judaism, which I address in sections 4.1 and 4.2, but first the diversity of divine movement in the Bible and its distinctive human involvement need attention. The most pervasive analogue to Baal's movement from mountain to city in Israelite tradition is YHWH's journey from Sinai to Jerusalem. Divine names including Sinai are not frequent in the Hebrew Bible, but do appear at Judges 5:5 and Psalm 68:8.[7] The starkest difference from the Baal tradition is the connection of the divine journey to the story of the Israelites escaping from Egypt and traveling to Mount Sinai, where they pick up this deity, build him a portable dwelling, and transport him to Canaan.[8] Between the arrival in this new location and the building of a permanent dwelling, the divine presence is connected to the ambiguous object called the ark of the covenant, most clearly associated with the place called Shiloh during part of the story. When the great kings, David and Solomon, complete the temple in Jerusalem, they bring this object to the city and place it

---

[5] See the presentation and discussion of these ancient tablets found at Ugarit in Michael D. Coogan and Mark S. Smith, eds. *Stories from Ancient Canaan*, 2nd ed. (Louisville, KY: Westminster John Knox, 2012), 97–153.

[6] Mark. S. Smith, *Where the Gods Are: Spatial Dimensions of Anthropomorphism in the Biblical World* (New Haven, CT: Yale University Press, 2016), 78–84.

[7] On Sinai as divine home and the appearance of this name, see Jon D. Levenson, *Sinai and Zion: An Entry into the Jewish Bible* (San Francisco, CA: Harper & Row, 1985), 19–23.

[8] This understanding of the process is most complete in the source document labeled Priestly (P), one of the four primary sources used to compose the Torah. It is now possible to read this source straight through, uninterrupted, thanks to the work of Seth E. Sanders at https://pentateuch.digital.

in the temple. The ark fades from view, but the divine presence abides in the temple there until the Babylonian destruction of the temple in the early sixth century forces it to depart, an event depicted most graphically in the vision of Ezekiel 8–10. The geographical instability the long story creates will be treated more extensively in Section 4 of this Element.

There is a separate kind of tradition in the Hebrew Bible in which YHWH travels on his own from the south to Jerusalem, in an act less connected to human events. The locations in this tradition, like Seir and Teman, also depict mountainous abodes. The more obscure records of Israel's God coming from these regions to Canaan to occupy the temple in Jerusalem are in poems like Judges 5 and Habakkuk 3 that appear to be among the oldest texts in the Hebrew Bible.[9] While Israel's God can be present in multiple places, the ancient abodes were a problem for scribal traditions increasingly incorporated into urban temples. When Elijah fled from Jezebel after his victory in the contest and returned to Horeb (the other name for Mount Sinai), there was some sort of divine presence there – but it was an ambiguous one, characterized primarily by silence – that compelled him to leave immediately (1 Kings 19:15). The dynamism and unpredictability of this deity made for great stories of the distant past but created challenges in the present of the scribes compiling the books of the Bible.

1.2 Forming an Israelite God

The God of the Bible goes through two massive, related transformations, one entirely inside the story world of the text and the other within both that world and the world producing the text. First, YHWH becomes less active and interventionist in human affairs. The transition from an active, interventionist god, like the one who creates and floods the world, destroys Sodom and Gomorra, and defeats Pharaoh with plagues and the manipulation of the sea, to the one who gently cultivates the spirit of Cyrus the Great to release the exiled people of Judah (Ezra 1:1) and sponsor their return to Jerusalem, may be the most underappreciated aspect of the biblical tradition. Second, this deity is progressively disembodied within the plot of the Bible. The disembodiment of YHWH has been documented most completely in the recent work of Francesca Stavrakopoulou, and it is related to the fitful progress toward a monotheistic presentation of God in the Bible. Demonstrating the process requires careful work with both texts and material remains.[10] It is also a process

---

[9] See the discussion in Smith, *Where the Gods Are*, 91–97.

[10] On these processes and the connections between them, see Francesca Stavrakopoulou, *God: An Anatomy* (New York: Knopf, 2022), 23–25.

Table 1 Divine designations in the Pentateuch

Divine designations	Number of occurrences	Locations
YHWH	1820 times	
Elohim	813 times (in various grammatical forms)	
YHWH *Elohim*	Used in combination 21 times	12 in Genesis 2, 8 in Genesis 3, and Exodus 9:30
`*El*	34 times	
`*Elyon*	2 times	Numbers 24:14 and Deuteronomy 32:8
`*El* `*Elyon*	4 times	all in Genesis 14
`*El Shaddai*	6 times	5 in Genesis, 1 in Exodus
`*El Ro'i*	1 time	Genesis 16:13
`*El 'olam*	1 time	Genesis 21:33
Yah	2 times	Exodus 15:2 and 17:16[12]

that had to be extended in both Jewish and Christian interpretation beyond the formation of the biblical canon.[11] The disembodied, quiet deity, operating inside human beings, is easier to portray in a consistent and singular way. Attention to these processes will appear in each of the following sections of this Element.

The simplest way to observe the diversity of divine portrayals in the Hebrew Bible is to catalogue the many designations used to name, identify, or address the deity. The designations in Table 1 are from the Pentateuch alone, the five books from Genesis to Deuteronomy.

At the conclusion of his masterful *God: A Biography*, Jack Miles responded to the multiplicity of names and personalities attributed to the deity of the Hebrew Bible with an effort to produce a "polytheistic retelling." In his own estimation the revision produced a story with a greater sense of calm and inevitability, rather than one focused on a single divine character who is rife with anxiety and unpredictability.[13] This textual anxiety reflects conflict among the traditions that came together to form ancient Israel and define its God. Miles's observations about the biblical God named YHWH and his troubled

---

[11] Ibid., 418–423.

[12] This apparently shortened form of the divine name is abundant in Psalms, especially in the familiar phrase *hallelu-Yah* ("Praise Yah").

[13] Jack Miles, *God: A Biography* (New York: Vintage, 1995), 398–402.

singularity reinvigorate questions about how such a character may have developed.

The harsh biblical rejection of Baal makes the Bible's reckoning with the Canaanite God named El remarkable and confusing. The foremost depiction of Israel's God as separate from, but related to, El is the stunning section of the Song of Moses in Deuteronomy 32:8–9, which declares that Elyon divided the land among nations to match "the number of the gods." Within this divine drama, Elyon matches YHWH, who is one of the second-level deities, with Israel ("Jacob"). There are considerable textual variations among ancient versions at this point, which is understandable given the theological stakes. The standardized (Masoretic) Hebrew text says "the number of the Israelites," which makes no sense. A fragment of a Deuteronomy scroll from Qumran reads "the number of the sons of God," and most Greek manuscripts read "the number of the angels of God." The text and its reception history demonstrate that the full identification of YHWH with the high God El was a long process. One of the greatest complications in the relationship between YHWH and El is that some texts depict Baal as a son of El.[14] Thus, when YHWH emerges as Israel's distinct deity, who can be equated with El, he also looks like his chief rival's father. Depictions of El in written texts and images typically show an elderly figure.[15] Stories of El and Baal often exhibit conflict between the two, and it may be that YHWH inherited the conflict with Baal by incorporating the identity of El. Mark Smith has proposed a three-stage historical process by which YHWH became identified with El. In the first stage El was Israel's original God, as the name of the group and an early worship site like Bethel ("House of El") demonstrate. In a second stage, YHWH was a warrior deity within a pantheon headed by El. In the final stage, the two were equated and the identity of El, along with the appearance of his name, became increasingly scarce.[16]

Smith and others can outline a process like this in part because of archaeological discoveries outside of the biblical text, but also because of traces left behind within the Bible. While there are plenty of signs that some parts of the Bible, and ways of reading it, attempted to erase the presence of a polytheistic past, there are other places where those traces remain. An extended narrative that presents Israel's God as a complex character developing during a long period of time makes it possible to see these diverse portrayals of deity as a single figure.

---

[14] Other texts describe Baal as the son of Dagan.

[15] For more on these depictions, see Mark S. Smith, *The Origins of Biblical Monotheism: Israel's Polytheistic Background and the Ugaritic Texts* (Oxford: Oxford University Press, 2001), 136.

[16] Ibid., 143–144.

1.3 Plan of This Element

If the presentation of monotheism in the Hebrew Bible is entwined with and dependent upon the plot in which its deity is a major character, then a careful outline of that plot and how the divine character appears in it is an essential beginning and will be the primary goal of Section 2. One surprising feature revealed by a careful review of divine characterization is that Israel's God ages. YHWH changes through the course of the plot, and these changes correspond in significant ways to the stages of an aging human character. Certain literary choices the composers of the biblical books made connected aspects of YHWH's life to specific points in a human life cycle, and Section 3 will observe how this life cycle fits the presentation of Israel's deity.

The idea that the victors write history is presented so often as a great axiom of human civilization that we may fail to notice and describe the ways in which the Hebrew Bible refutes it. The emergence of this literary collection from a long series of experiences of defeat and destruction presents particular difficulties for the portrayal of the deity to whom Israelite tradition eventually declared complete loyalty. Section 4 will explore the ways the literature of the Hebrew Bible presents an emerging monotheism as a way of surviving the trauma of a devastating sequence of events in the human world.

The deity in the early parts of the plot of the Hebrew Bible could hardly be more different than the one most modern readers presume to encounter. The more difficult question related to this issue is how the ancient deity compared to the one the biblical writers understood. The final section of this Element will compare these three points of perception and portrayal of the divine character. How are the God of Israel's most ancient traditions related to the deity of the scribes who produced the biblical books, and how do each of those relate to the gods of various modern readers? Finally, how does the concept of monotheism map onto that long story of God in the text and in that world that has so long attended to that text? The God of the most famous parts of the Hebrew Bible – creation, exodus, and the settling of Canaan – is not the kind of deity modern people experience. In its formative period, biblical scholarship came to describe the defining behaviors of Israel's deity as "the mighty acts of God." Even at the end of the story the Hebrew Bible tells, however, God is not a mighty actor, but a quiet, invisible figure not unlike the modern perception.

2 God in the Plot of the Hebrew Bible

The basic plot of the Hebrew Bible is familiar to many people, but a careful explanation of how and where it appears, accompanied by specific attention to the changing presentation of the divine character within it, is necessary in the development of this Element. The sequence of books that opens the Hebrew Bible, beginning with Genesis and ending with Kings, tells a continuous story from the creation of the world to the destruction of Jerusalem by the Babylonian Empire of Nebuchadnezzar in the early sixth century. The book(s) known as Chronicles presents this basic plot again, though the presence and absence of certain details give the story a different character and prioritize different ideas. A combination of genealogies, birth and death notices, and royal chronologies, all of which are literary artifacts with widely varying relations to the modern notion of history, depict this as a story that lasts about two and a half millennia. After a gap of several decades, the book called Ezra-Nehemiah picks up this narrative and carries it into the fifth century BCE. The remaining books of the Hebrew Bible attach themselves to this plot at various places and view the events from varying perspectives. In many cases the relative dates of composition of these texts do not match the narrative order of the events recorded, so the concerns of writers and their audiences may shape the presentations differently. Outside of the narrow collection of books in the Hebrew Bible, the story is continued and retold in the Maccabean literature and the works of Philo and Josephus, but the development of Israelite traditions concerning YHWH had largely achieved fixed status for this deity as the one God of the universe within the Hebrew Bible. Several ways in which this narrative character developed within the text helped contribute to this sense of a single deity, despite divergent characterizations. As the previous section indicated, events in the life of this deity are often connected to events in the human realm, so it is necessary to trace the plot of that combined human–divine story to see what its God looks like and how he behaves.

2.1 Creation of the Universe

Texts portraying the creative activity of ancient Israel's deity in Genesis 1–3, Isaiah (primarily chapters 40, 45, and 51), a handful of Psalms (8, 74, 89, and 104), Job 38–41, and Proverbs 8 vary in their perspectives and styles. God can be a warrior deity doing battle with monsters that inflict chaos upon the world.[17] Readers can catch glimpses of this kind of battle, such as in Psalm 74:12–17, but it has been greatly suppressed in the biblical tradition, in favor of a divine being characterized more by the power of speech and the skilled crafting of the world.[18]

---

[17] On the connections between this type of portrayal in the Bible and its larger context in the ancient Mediterranean world, see Gregory Mobley, *The Return of the Chaos Monsters* (Grand Rapids, MI: Eerdmans, 2012), 16–19.

[18] For a thorough discussion and comparison of these texts and the way they present the divine creator, see Mark S. Smith, *The Priestly Vision of Genesis 1* (Minneapolis, MN: Fortress, 2010), 11–37.

These are the characterizations that come through most powerfully in Genesis 1–3, and their presence at the beginning of the Bible provides them with an influence far beyond their size. It is difficult for readers not to read all other texts in the Bible through the lens of Genesis 1–3.

The divine portrayals in Genesis 1 and 2 famously differ, but in both the deity manages the materials of creation, through either speech, the manipulation of matter, or both. The variation in divine designations between Elohim in Genesis 1:1–2:4a and YHWH Elohim in 2:4b–3:24 is perhaps the most noticeable difference, but there are many more subtle ones. In Genesis 1 God mostly speaks, seemingly at a distance from the world he is creating. In Genesis 2–3 God touches the world and the humans he creates, and he walks around on the ground with them. The transcendent deity of Genesis 1 is not completely disembodied, if speech requires body parts, but the extent of the divine anthropomorphism is strikingly different. The deity of Genesis 2–3 also has direct conversation with humans who speak back to him, enhancing the human characterization of God. This is accompanied by an emphasis on the movement of humans toward godlike status (3:23). Each of the two accounts in which God is making the environment and the creatures that live within it have a corresponding account of the flood in Genesis 6–8, in which the deity controls the weather and uses it to punish the perceived failures of humanity. Again, the differing divine designations, Elohim in one story and YHWH in the other, is a distinguishing feature.[19] Even though these deities have different names and operate in different ways, they are doing the same basic things, and readers have long assumed they are one being.

In the "Primeval" portion of Genesis (chapters 1–11) the deity does a lot of talking, at first to the material world and the general collections of living things, including humans, that inhabit it, and then to some of the specific human characters. These human characters sometimes respond in speech to God but rarely, if ever, do the humans talk to each other. The deity is the primary speaker. The human characters become more talkative in the stories of the great ancestors beginning in Genesis 12 and they are often in dialogue with each other, but the divine character is still a frequent speaker. The next section will address this shift in characterization more substantially.

---

[19] These two divine designations are challenging to render adequately in English. The Hebrew word *Elohim* is plural in form but can be used to designate an individual deity or multiple deities. When used for divine characters other than Israel's God it is often difficult to tell whether it is singular or plural. This is not a name for God, but is not quite a common noun when referring to Israel's deity. It is closer to a title. The specific name for Israel's deity that eventually dominates the biblical plot is not pronounced in Jewish tradition, so it comes without its own vowels in the Hebrew text. The all-consonant rendering YHWH will appear most often in this Element. The common English translation of this name as LORD is problematic because it is an authoritative title that sounds odd in the mouth of foreigners who do not worship this deity.

The deity of the Genesis creation accounts is not alone. He speaks in first-person plural language in 1:26, 3:22, and 11:7. Genesis 6:1–4 tells the story of a group of divine beings called "the sons of God," who go down to earth and impregnate human women, creating a race of semidivine giants. Ancient Jewish literature that parallels Genesis, like 1 Enoch and Jubilees, portrays and names a plethora of divine beings, including a large group led by Shemihazah who instructs humans in the development of material culture, a band of archangels (Michael, Sariel, Raphael, and Gabriel) who carry out divine missions, and a group of spirits led by Mastema who mislead the offspring of Noah after the flood. There is always a crowd around Israel's God, but their status is inconsistent and unclear. First Enoch and Jubilees did not make their way into the limited collection that became the Hebrew Scriptures, and it is tempting to see this pantheon as one of the features that might have made these texts problematic. Most Christian formulations of the "Old Testament" also left out these two books and their more visible pantheons.[20]

A different kind of divine accompaniment appears in creation traditions like Proverbs 8 and a similar text in Sirach 24.[21] In these poems a feminine character identified as "Wisdom" speaks of being the first of God's creations and then assisting him in the remainder of creation, including human beings. One of the features of Proverbs that makes the book difficult is its lack of connection to the core traditions of the Israelite story. It contains no mention of the great ancestors, the exodus, or the encounter at Sinai. Sirach 24 seeks to fix this difficulty using the Wisdom figure. The most significant move in this poem is the equation of Wisdom with the law given by Moses. Accompanying this connection is the placement of the Jordan, Israel's river, among the four great Mesopotamian and African rivers from Genesis 2. Linking universal forces and entities to specifically Israelite ones brought the broader diversity of divine understanding under greater control, giving it more defined geography and a more specific representation in the human world. Whether Wisdom is a goddess, and whether she is the consort of Israel's God, is a matter of disagreement, but her persistence in these traditions adds to the complexity of the divine entourage in the Hebrew Bible.[22]

---

[20] Jubilees and 1 Enoch were only preserved in the canon of the Ethiopian Orthodox Church and its Ge'ez language, but extensive fragmentary remains of both works among the Dead Sea Scrolls demonstrated their presence within Second Temple Judaism.

[21] Sirach is not in the Hebrew Bible but is present in the Old Testament of Roman Catholic and Orthodox Christianity. A fragment found among the Dead Sea Scrolls has strengthened the case that it was preserved in Hebrew and had a place within Second Temple Judaism.

[22] On the similarities of YHWH's creation of this figure to other traditions in the ancient world, especially Atum's creation of Shu and Tetnat in Egyptian tradition, see Stavrakopoulou, *God: An Anatomy*, 120–125.

The development of written texts as divine representations was an additional stage in this process, which will receive more attention later in this section.

The deity in Genesis 1–11 is not related to the Israelites alone, because they have not yet been defined in the plot. The relation between YHWH, who is not yet Israel's distinctive deity, and the mysterious figure named Nimrod in Genesis 10:8–12, is strange and captivating. This gigantic figure, associated with Cush/Ethiopia by birth and credited with building the great cities of ancient Mesopotamia, like Babel and Nineveh, is the first to be "a great *gibbor* before YHWH." In the story of the people of Babel in Genesis 11:1–9, YHWH responds to and controls the actions of these members of a Mesopotamian civilization. The continuing story of Israel's deity faces a two-edged difficulty as the influential set of stories that begins the Bible comes to a close with a genealogy that carries the story from the family of Noah to the appearance of Abram/Abraham. How can this universal deity be the specific God of Israel, and how can this national deity be the one God of the universe? A large collection of texts with a coherent overall plot is well suited to bring disparate characterizations together and attempt to resolve these questions.

2.2 God of the Ancestors

At Genesis 11:27 the Hebrew Bible's mode of storytelling shifts dramatically. The human characters become much more highly developed when the one-dimensional likes of Adam, Eve, Cain, Noah, and Shem give way to Abraham, Sarah, Hagar, Isaac, Rebekkah, Jacob, Rachel, Leah, and Joseph, characters whose hopes, dreams, struggles, and disappointments are visible. The vague geography of Eden, Nod, Ararat, and Shinar are replaced by Shechem, Bethel, Beersheba, and Gilgal, locations likely familiar to the earliest audiences of Genesis and locatable on modern maps. The deity in Genesis 12–50 is intimately tied to these human characters and precise earthly places, but this shifting spatiality is a problem the collecting and shaping of traditions by scribes would eventually need to address.

The discussion of creation identified the variation of names for the divine character used by the narrators as one of the factors biblical scholars use to divide this Genesis material into sources. The divine character receives no fewer than ten names in the first five books of the Bible (see the list in Table 1), but there is a definite trend toward the use of the distinctive divine name, YHWH, revealed to Moses in Exodus 3.[23] Translation into modern languages and reading practices may keep readers from noticing this variation, and in the

---

[23] See the discussion of these names and patterns of distribution in Mark McEntire, *Portraits of a Mature God: Choices in Old Testament Theology* (Minneapolis, MN: Fortress, 2013), 58–60.

ancestral narratives there continue to be places where it is difficult to be certain
how we are to know that this is all one character. The famous *Akedah* ("binding"
of Isaac) story is a good example. When the "Angel of YHWH" appears in
Genesis 22:11–12 and halts the plan initiated by Elohim to kill the child, the
angel even says, "Now I know that you fear Elohim." The Angel of YHWH
makes a typical transformation into YHWH himself as the story progresses,
highlighting the tension between Elohim and YHWH. How are readers to
discern a single divine character? This may have proved difficult for some
ancient readers. The version of this story that appears in Jubilees 17 has
Mastema, the ambiguous angel, instigating the command to Abraham to kill
his son, while the divine character intervenes later to stop it.[24] The Akedah story
is famously malleable in terms of where it happens – Moriah, Jerusalem,
Gerazim – and in terms of who the boy is – Isaac or Ishmael – and it is also
malleable in its identification of the villain who initiates the test.

One of the important places where the different divine manifestations are
unified is in the second encounter between God and Moses, in which the deity
says, "I appeared to Abraham, Isaac, and Jacob as El Shaddai, but by my name,
YHWH, I did not make myself known to them" (Exodus 6:3). El Shaddai is one
of several "El-____" designations for Israel's God in the Bible. The discussion
in Section 1 pointed to the poem in Deuteronomy 32 that makes a distinction
between Elyon (sometimes El Elyon) and YHWH, making YHWH a second-
level deity who is assigned to the nation of Israel. The Moses tradition in Exodus
6 is an important part of the effort to complete the fusion of Israel's distinct god
and the high god of Canaanite culture, but the human characters in the story are
related to the divine character in shifting and complex ways.

The stories of the ancestors and the exodus are also made up of a combination
of interwoven sources that name the divine character differently at various
points in the plot. For example, it is Elohim who renames Jacob during the
nocturnal wrestling match of Genesis 32:22–32, and the name of El appears in
both Jacob's new name "Israel" (El strives) and the name that Jacob gives to the
place, "Peniel" (Face of El). In the other version of the renaming in 35:9–15,
Elohim gives Jacob the name Israel but identifies himself as El Shaddai. In
Jacob's initial divine encounter in 28:10–17, Jacob refers to the divine character
as YHWH but names the place of that encounter Bethel (house of El). This
mixture of divine designation is both confusing and confirming. For the scribes
who compiled all of these sources into the Torah, these are all references to
Israel's one God.

---

[24] The plot in Jubilees 17 sounds similar to the beginning of the book of Job, with a heavenly
adversarial figure encouraging the divine character to test the faithfulness of a human character.

In the book of Genesis alone it is possible to see a profound transition in the divine portrayal by looking at the way God interacts with the primary characters in the book. God speaks directly to early characters like Adam, Eve, Cain, and Noah, without any theophanic fanfare. The conversations just begin. God also speaks directly to Abraham, Sarah, and Hagar, but some of these stories require narrative lead-in, such as initial angelic mediation or the facilitation of ritual like the flaying of animals by Abraham in Genesis 15. God speaks directly to Jacob sometimes but also appears to him in dreams. By the end of the book, however, in the long story of Joseph (Genesis 39–50), God no longer speaks directly, and even the dreams of Joseph do not contain direct divine communication. Instead, they are symbolic dreams requiring interpretation.[25] This trend sees a strong reversal early in the Exodus story when God summons Moses from the burning bush and begins a long series of divine appearances and direct conversations. Narrative framing is still necessary most of the time, as Moses must go up the mountain or into the sacred tent to speak with God.

The exodus story holds out the possibility of a more direct interaction with the divine character for all Israelites, but that plan goes awry in Exodus 19–20. The God of Sinai turns out to be more fearsome and dangerous than expected. One wrong step in this deity's presence could lead to death. In the famous Ten Commandments story in Exodus 20, it seems as if all the people hear the voice of God reciting the series of regulations, a list that does not sound particularly onerous. As soon as the recital is finished, however, the people express unbearable terror and beg Moses to be their intermediary: "You speak to us, and we will listen; but do not let God speak to us or we will die" (Exodus 20:19). For the remainder of the Torah, this is the pattern in all legal texts. Either YHWH is speaking to Moses (sometimes accompanied by Aaron the High Priest), as in the entire book of Leviticus, or Moses is reporting divine commands to the people, as in the book of Deuteronomy.

The relationships among the people, the mountain, and the deity who seems to dwell there require ongoing negotiation and redefinition. Kenneth Ngwa's Africana reading of the exodus traditions insists that "The Mountain . . . is not the site of exodus imagination or origin; it is preeminently the colonial and imperial structure that needs exodus redesign work."[26] It is a reminder that the construction of monotheism threatens to be a colonial enterprise, which is another reason to avoid strict evolutionary assumptions about the development of monotheism. The continuing work of liberation, which the story of the

---

[25] For a fuller explication of this development, see W. Lee Humphreys, *The Character of God in the Book of Genesis* (Louisville, KY: Westminster John Knox, 2001).

[26] Kenneth N. Ngwa, *Let My People Live: An Africana Reading of Exodus* (Louisville, KY: Westminster John Knox, 2022), 156.

exodus seems to be about, sometimes requires the disruption of monotheistic patterns of belief. Such is the case, for example, when what Yung Suk Kim calls "exclusive monotheism" develops on the basis of race and ethnicity.[27] The development of ideas about God in ancient Israel, which often receives the label monotheism, was always entangled with the development of group and national identity. Those who constructed these divine and human identities were claiming power, and the continuing story of Israel and its God remained a contested one.

2.3 God of the Nation

When the story of Israel continues beyond the Torah, there are almost always professional intermediaries present to facilitate divine communication, from Joshua to Samuel to Elijah and beyond. Eventually, the role of prophet emerges and matures as the primary conduit for divine communication. A few prophets early in this development also perform miracles. Elijah calls down divine fire on the top of Mount Carmel and raises to life the dead son of a widow in Zarephath. Elisha helps to cure the leprosy of a Syrian military commander and summons bears from the woods to slaughter some rude children. Isaiah facilitates the healing of King Hezekiah and the backward movement of a shadow. Eventually, the declaration of the word of YHWH becomes the primary, or only, kind of prophetic work, and later these words are used to produce written scrolls that carry on the tradition of these prophets beyond their human lives. Scribal work became an additional layer of mediation between God and God's people. This process demonstrates how the divine presence became increasingly removed from the experience of humans.

The character named Samuel is an important transitional figure in the plot of the Hebrew Bible. Sometimes he looks like a political leader, similar to the "judge" characters who precede him in the story. He also performs the functions of a priest, attending to the sanctuary in Shiloh and conducting sacrificial rituals. Most importantly, he is a prophet who divines the will of God and anoints the initial kings of Israel and Judah. Once these kings are in place and begin to build a temple and sponsor a priesthood, the divining role becomes separate and is the exclusive task of prophets, who are sometimes antagonistic toward kings and priests. The divine character is ambivalent about this developing division of labor. In 1 Samuel 8, YHWH begrudgingly allows the Israelites to choose a king but feels rejected and delineates the negative effects of kingship in a way that sounds like punishment in response to this human desire for power. The kings that follow sometimes receive divine favor but can also face rejection and

---

[27] Yung Suk Kim, *Monotheism, Biblical Traditions, and Race Relations* (Cambridge: Cambridge University Press, 2022), 3–6.

defeat. The stories of the nations of Israel and Judah end in destruction. The national tragedies will serve as a challenge to ancient Israel's understanding of its God but will ultimately provide the pathway toward a monotheistic future. Section 5 of this Element will describe that process more thoroughly.

The way the divine character appears in the four big scrolls called the "prophetic literature" varies, of course. Divine speech is often difficult to characterize because it is fused in different ways with the speech of the prophet. In places like Isaiah 6:9–13 and 8:1–15, the first-person voice of Isaiah ben Amoz introduces YHWH as a speaker, and the reader encounters that divine speech; but it is more difficult to determine who is speaking and how in a place like Isaiah 9:1–7. In the book of Isaiah, and even Isaiah ben Amoz himself, eventually disappears, and prophetic speech has little or no narrative framing. The situation is different in Ezekiel, which is more consistent in its framing. The first-person voice of Ezekiel persists almost to the end of the book and reports divine speech he receives. Interaction between the prophet and the audience is far less common. The prophetic literature in the Hebrew Bible invites the reader to assume a mechanism in which the prophet receives speech from YHWH then reports it to an audience, but the content of the speech is never repeated twice. Each of the scrolls does this differently and includes different kinds of exceptions to this pattern. The book of Jeremiah, for example, includes a series of conversations between the prophet and YHWH, embedded in Jeremiah 11–20 that are more personal in nature. These are often labeled Jeremiah's laments or confessions, because he is expressing his own doubt and confusion about the effects of his prophetic work. There is little narrative framing of this divine–human conversation, and no implication that some audience contemporary to Jeremiah himself heard a report from the prophet. Rather, these poems seem developed to function within a written book, with readers/hearers as the audience.

The prophetic scrolls both record and enact an understanding of deity. In early parts of the scroll of Isaiah, a distinct human personality has direct encounters with a speaking deity. Isaiah ben Amoz says, "I saw YHWH" (6:1). A much later tradition, recorded in the first century work *The Martyrdom of Isaiah*, has King Manasseh of Judah put Isaiah on trial for this statement, which seems blasphemous in later times, and execute him by sawing him in two when he refuses to recant. By the end of the book of Isaiah, human and divine bodies and personalities have largely dissolved, and poetic speeches beginning with prophetic formulae, like "Thus says YHWH" and "Hear the word of YHWH" appear in disorienting sequence with no narrative context. The scroll of Ezekiel begins with a grand theophanic vision, from which YHWH speaks to the prophet. It ends with an elaborate vision of a rebuilt temple and city of Jerusalem. The prophet goes into the vision, where his tour is guided by an angelic figure. Divine speeches, introduced by prophetic formulae, are embedded within the vision. It is difficult to see how this could ever have functioned as anything other than a written text.

This withdrawal of direct divine presence is carefully negotiated in a strange and anxious little story in the book of Haggai, near the end of Book of the Twelve. Haggai was a prophet in the postexilic period who is present as a character in the book of Ezra during the stories of the rebuilding of the temple. The book of Haggai contains four prophetic oracles that seem related to the same time period, each with some narrative framework. The presentation fluctuates, with some confusion, between Haggai's delivery of the divine message, "the word of YHWH came by the prophet Haggai" (1:3 and 2:1), and his reception of the divine speech, "the word of YHWH came to Haggai" (2:20). The confusion occurs because the divine message in 2:10–19 asks questions of the priests and requires their interaction to proceed. The written text accomplishes this awkwardly by having the priests interact with Haggai's reception of the divine message, producing a scene only possible in the imagination of the reader. The transition from the prophet as a human figure mediating the divine presence for a listening audience to the prophetic scroll mediating the divine presence by reporting the work of a prophet as a literary figure was an intricate development that did not always produce smooth results.

The way in which the divine character is named, designated, or addressed varies in the prophetic scrolls, but the divine name YHWH dominates, with the more general Elohim making up most of the rest. Beyond this common name and a relation to the people of Israel, how is the reader to perceive this divine character who interacts with different prophets in different places in different ways as the same figure? One of the ways that happens is by way of the slim, but definite, connections between these prophetic scrolls and the long story of Israel described in chapter 2. At the beginnings of these scrolls and at certain points within them, brief "superscriptions" appear, which say things like, "The word of YHWH that came to Hosea son of Beeri, in the days of King Uzziah, Jotham, Ahaz, and Hezekiah of Judah, and in the days of Jeroboam son of Joash of Israel" (Hosea 1:1). The prophetic scrolls thus assume some awareness with the stories of Israel and Judah and their succession of monarchs. The story of Israel and the story of its God help hold each other together.

2.4 The Development of Israel as a Nation Outside the Bible

Over recent decades, archaeological evidence has accumulated to support a near consensus conclusion that Israel and Judah began as separate social and political entities. They combined when the neo-Assyrian Empire largely destroyed Israel and its capital in Samaria toward the end of the eighth century BCE. Many of the dispersed survivors made their way south and became part of Judah. The northerners brought with them traditions that scribes eventually combined with the traditions of Judah, and it is this combination readers now see in many parts of the Bible. The fusion of northern and southern traditions to create a story that projected their developing unity back into the distant past is visible in multiple places but is essential to understand in two periods of the story the Hebrew Bible tells. First, the book of Genesis combines the stories of the great southern ancestors, Abraham and Sarah, with the great northern ancestors, Jacob and his family. Second, the book(s) called Samuel bring together the first northern king, Saul, and the first great chief/king of Judah, David. The books now known as 1 and 2 Samuel present Saul, David, and Solomon as great kings of a unified nation in the distant past. Traditional study of the Bible often labels this era "the United Monarchy." In both cases it is not completely clear how the deities of these separate political entities were related to each other and what had to happen in the telling of the stories to move them toward a single identity. Careful examination of a few important texts may reveal some of the broader contours of that development.

One of the oddities created by the joining of these traditions is that Genesis contains no stories that include Abraham and Jacob together, even though the chronology of the book has Abraham dying when Jacob is fourteen years old. This lacuna was seemingly repaired in the book of Jubilees, which portrays several interactions between the famous grandfather and grandson pair.[28]

The stories in the Hebrew Bible of Abraham, Sarah, and Hagar take place primarily in what is now perceived as the southern part of Israel, in places like Beersheba, Mamre/Hebron, the Negeb, Kadesh, and Gerar. The deity with whom they interact is most often YHWH, but is also Elohim, El Elyon, El Olam, El Roi, and El Shaddai. The stories in Genesis about Jacob and his family are primarily located in the northern part of Israel, in places like Bethel, Mizpah, Peniel, Shechem, and Gilead. The deity with whom Jacob and his family interact is most often YHWH, but can be Elohim, El, El-Bethel, El Shaddai, and El-Elohe-Israel. Isaac and Rebekkah are difficult figures because they serve primarily to connect Abraham to Jacob, and there is relatively little separate material about them. They are most closely associated with the southern location called Beersheba. Despite the brevity of Isaac's traditions, there is one

---

[28] Comparisons of divine designations in Jubilees are problematic because only fragments of the Hebrew text remain and the book has only been fully preserved in Ethiopic, and this version was likely produced from a Greek translation. In the stories of Abraham and Jacob together, which are unique to Jubilees, the designation usually translated "God Most High" dominates. See the translation of James C. VanderKam, *Jubilees* (Minneapolis, MN: Fortress, 2020), 79–83.

unique divine designation that appears there, "the Fear of Isaac" (Genesis 31:42 and 53), as it is usually translated. It is also in the Isaac material that the phrase "God of Abraham" first appears (28:13). The phrase is paired with "God of Isaac" here as YHWH identifies himself to Jacob at Bethel. "God of Abraham" also appears near both occurrences of "Fear of Isaac" in Genesis 31. In the famous burning bush encounter of Moses, the full formula naming all three patriarchs, "The God of your ancestors, the God of Abraham, the God of Isaac, and the God of Jacob," finally appears. The biblical narrative has succeeded by this point in joining all of these divine traditions together. It is much more difficult to say how they became joined in the story outside the biblical text, where these characters were likely independent of one another.

The variety of these traditions likely indicates that the coalescing of the divine figures associated with these human characters followed along with the process of joining together of ancient Israel as a family, twelve tribes of people, each named for one of the twelve sons of Jacob. The books known as Joshua and Judges help illustrate the difficulty of developing a clear picture of this history. Most of the book of Joshua presents a unified picture of the Israelites moving into the land of Canaan and conquering it, with YHWH giving instructions to the character named Joshua, who leads the Israelites accordingly. The book of Judges shows the Israelites operating as individual tribes or small clusters of tribes struggling to take and hold territory in the Levant amid conflict with a variety of territorial enemies. The idea of a unified ancient Israel in the distant past is a literary artifact, but even in literary terms it is not the only way of remembering. Outside the Bible, the ancient Israelites emerged from Canaanite culture as the Bronze Age political structures collapsed, leaving space for new ways of living and understanding group identity.[29]

The biblical story first brings Saul and David together in 1 Samuel 16, when David comes into Saul's court to be his musician and armor bearer. Saul and David have two more initial encounters in the story of David and Goliath in 1 Samuel 17. Adding to the confusion is that 16:18 describes David as "a man of valor, a warrior," while 17:12–18 describes David as a boy too young to be in the army, whom his father sends to the scene of the battle to take food to his older brothers. After David has killed Goliath he brings the giant's head to Saul, who does not know who David is. The awkwardness of three different first meetings of the two figures likely indicates that traditions had brought them together in different ways that had become established firmly enough to necessitate including them in the book of Samuel. Saul's divine encounters, mediated

---

[29] For a description of this phenomenon throughout the Mediterranean world as the Bronze Age came to an end and the Iron Age began, see Eric H. Cline, 1177 *B.C.: The Year Civilization Collapsed* (Princeton, NJ: Princeton University Press, 2014), 171–176.

by Samuel, occur in places like Mizpah, Shechem, and Gilgal, important locations in the northern nation of Israel. David's mostly occur in southern locations like Hebron and Jerusalem. When the book of Samuel brings these two together, the process of anointing kings is at the center of the story, and the prophet named Samuel anoints both of them, multiple times.

The Bible we have is a product of Judah, with traditions from Israel embedded within it for different purposes. The subordination of Israel is apparent in the subordination of the northern heroes, Jacob and Saul, to the southern ones, Abraham and David. Eventually, the southern political and religious center of Jerusalem comes to dominate our perception of the biblical story. Nevertheless, the whole narrative is dependent on Israelite traditions in many ways. As Daniel Fleming has expressed it, "Somehow, the eventual survivors of Judah, long after the kingdom of Israel had failed, considered that their own history was best told in terms of this neighbor, with whom they understood themselves to be deeply connected."[30] It may have been that their conceptions of deity were part of this connection, but it also meant that a much broader collection of portrayals of that deity needed to come together in the telling of the story in ways that created a credible sense of the same God.

2.5 Unique Presentations of Divine Behavior

The divine speech in Job 38–42 requires unique attention. The book of Job might attach itself to the larger biblical narrative plot as a microcosm of the national experiences of exile and restoration, told as the story of one family, but the setting of the book, in terms of both time and place, is ambiguous. A speaking deity would not be out of place in a tale from the distant past, and the lack of specific references to time and place in Job allows the readers' imaginations to place the story there. Job himself resembles characters like Abraham and Jacob. On the other hand, this speaking deity is unlike any other whom readers of the Bible encounter. First, Job must badger his God into speech throughout thirty-five chapters of dialogue with his friends, all of whom seem to think they speak for God. They are shocked into silence when God begins to speak and are never heard from again. Second, God does not speak to Job so much as at him, in a barrage of rhetorical questions that sound like intimidation. The character of the deity, one who not only speaks like this to a human but makes wagers with lesser divine beings about that human's loyalty, looks as much outside the sequence of the biblical narrative as the setting of Job is outside Israel's story. Understanding this as the same God depicted elsewhere in

---

[30] Daniel E. Fleming, *The Legacy of Israel in Judah's Bible: History, Politics, and the Reinscribing of Tradition* (Cambridge: Cambridge University Press, 2012), 7.

the Bible has demanded work on the part of everyone involved in the produc-
tion, transmission, and reception of these traditions, and the sense of tension it
creates is still present. The incongruities and tensions of the book are expressed
well in the recent translation of the book by Edward Greenstein, which takes
seriously the notion, strange to the modern mind, that Job initiates and pursues
a lawsuit against his God.[31]

The idea of God that Job rails against is the one familiar in much of the Hebrew
Bible. Biblical scholarship has labeled this view "retribution theology." It says that
God rewards obedience with blessings and punishes disobedience with curses.
A clear and dramatic presentation of this idea appears in Deuteronomy 27–28,
where Moses commands the people to write down the curses and blessings on
plastered stones, after they have crossed the Jordan into Canaan, and set them atop
two opposing mountains. What Job and readers of the book know, and his friends in
dialogue with him inside the book do not know, is that the curses that have beset
him are not a sign that he has been disobedient. Gustavo Guttiérrez has argued that
the book of Job reasserts the freedom of God by resisting the mechanistic notions of
reward and punishment so common in other parts of the Hebrew Bible.[32] More
recently, C. L. Seow has taken a similar position, with careful attention to the divine
speech in Job 40–41, especially the introduction of the creatures named Rahab and
Leviathan. Seow describes YHWH's speech about the latter as "a veritable dox-
ology to Leviathan." YHWH has not subdued these forces of chaos but allows
them to have their way with humans. "The chaos monster is left untamed, ever
dangerous."[33] The claim that YHWH is capable of controlling such a monster but
does not do it leaves Job the human in a terrible position. He has received his divine
encounter and cannot respond, even though it is so thoroughly unsatisfying. The
restoration of Job's fortunes in the final chapter of the book calls this divine
reorientation into question. Is a deity who does not reward obedience and loyalty
too unpredictable and capricious to be useful to humans? The adjustments of
monotheistic belief to accommodate destruction and loss on a collective and
national scale will be the subject of Section 4 in this Element.

The book of Esther, in its Hebrew version, is famous for its lack of any direct
reference to Israel's deity. A major question surrounding the book's interpretation is whether this reticence is itself a way of presenting God. There are
multiple Greek versions of the book with additions that seek to present God
more overtly. They do this primarily through long, pious prayers offered by the

---

[31] See Edward L. Greenstein, *Job: A New Translation* (New Haven, CT: Yale University Press, 2019), xxi–xxviii.

[32] Gustavo Guttiérrez, *On Job: God-Talk and the Suffering of the Innocent* (Maryknoll, NY: Orbis, 1987), 67–81.

[33] C. L. Seow, *Job 1–21: Interpretation and Commentary* (Grand Rapids, MI: Eerdmans, 2013), 104.

major characters of the book. Most modern translations of the Bible reflect the shorter Hebrew version, and if they have the additions at all they are placed in the "Apocrypha" section, between the Old and New Testaments. While God is visibly present in the longer version of the book formed by the additions, this is a visualization created by the language of the characters. They address God as "king" and recall God's work with the great ancestors of the past like Abraham, but leave unchanged a basic premise of the book, that the faithful action of human heroes, operating in foreign, imperial contexts, are necessary to save the Jewish people from peril. The people fight their own battles, without the help of an interventionist God to knock down walls, send plagues onto enemies, or stop the sun.[34] Whether a character's absence in a narrative is a deliberate means of characterization is difficult to say. When that character's presence is so expected, and the absence so troubling, that subsequent versions of the story emerge that bring the character into the story in overt ways, the absence in the earlier story feels like a characterization that some readers wanted to contest. Megan Strollo has taken up these kinds of questions about divine behavior in all five of the little books that comprise the *Megilloth* in Jewish tradition – Ruth, Song of Songs, Ecclesiastes, Esther, and Lamentations. She is particularly concerned with the tension in these texts between divine inactivity and human agency. "[T]here is skepticism regarding the deity's inactivity, though it appears on a spectrum of sorts – ranging from doubt to seemingly indifferent silence to frustration and vehement protest. In addition, traditional theological convictions are reconsidered and challenged in each of these books and earlier traditions are called to account, questioned, and even recycled for new purposes."[35] These kinds of experiences and questions, located in books of the Bible that probably developed during the turmoil of the Second Temple Period, likely connect more clearly to modern human experience than the portrayals of the divine in the bigger, more famous books of the Hebrew Bible.

2.6 Summary of Divine Character Development

The reduction of YHWH's speaking role in the plot of the Hebrew Bible happens three times. First, in Genesis the divine character who speaks frequently to many different human characters but is silent for the last fifteen chapters of the book. Second, the divine character who reemerges to speak to Moses in Exodus 3, who sometimes speaks also to Aaron, and occasionally speaks to larger groups of Israelites in Exodus–Numbers, gives way to the voice

---

[34] See further discussion of Esther and its place in Jewish literature of the period in Mark McEntire, *An Apocryphal God: Beyond Divine Maturity* (Minneapolis, MN: Fortress, 2015), 86–89.

[35] Megan Fullerton Strollo, *Theologies of Human Agency: Counterbalancing Divine In/Activity in the Megilloth* (New York: Lexington Books, 2022), 75.

of Moses that dominates the book of Deuteronomy. Third, the divine character who emerges again after the end of the Torah to speak to Joshua, David, Solomon, Elijah, Isaiah, Jeremiah, Ezekiel, Jonah, and others does not speak to Ezra or Nehemiah.

The change in narrative depiction of Israel's God has received the most direct attention in Richard Elliot Friedman's *The Disappearance of God: A Divine Mystery*, in which he lists eight stages of the trajectory of divine presence:

1. Moses sees God at Sinai.
2. Moses, the one man who has seen God, wears a veil.
3. God tells Moses, "I shall hide my face from the Israelites."
4. The last time God is said to be revealed to a human: Samuel.
5. The last time God is said to have appeared to a human: King Solomon.
6. The last public miracle: divine fire for Elijah at Mount Carmel.
7. The last personal miracle: The shadow reverses before Isaiah and Hezekiah.
8. God is not mentioned in Esther.[36]

It is important to note that this sequence does not address divine communication with and appearances to prophets in the prophetic scrolls, but the discussion in section 2.3 demonstrated that these scrolls possess their own sense of increasing layers of mediation of divine presence. Friedman also attempted to put these eight stages and their texts in the order they may have been written, but these results are more speculative, and the narrative development of divine characterization is the more central question here. Nevertheless, in this process he offered a mechanism for this development that may be useful to ponder. The scribal processes that built the books of the Bible, moved them toward authoritative status, and formed them into a canonical order was too long, complex, and multifaceted to have had a deliberate and thorough strategy. Still, a deliberate tactic on the part of many, or most, of the scribes who did this work that pushed the more active portrayals of God into the distant past, away from the more recent events that reflected their own experience of a subtle, hidden God, could have produced this broad, general sense of movement.[37]

One dramatic demonstration of this narrative shift is visible in the stories of YHWH delivering the Israelites from Egypt in Exodus 7–15 and YHWH's deliverance of the exiled Judahites in Ezra 1–6, allowing them to return and rebuild Jerusalem. The same divine character who pummeled Pharaoh into submission over and over again, only to harden his heart so the lopsided contest

---

[36] Richard Elliott Friedman, *The Disappearance of God: A Divine Mystery* (Boston, MA: Little, Brown, 1995), 79–89.

[37] Friedman, *The Disappearance of God*, 88–89. See the discussion of this idea in McEntire, *Portraits of a Mature God*, 8–10.

could continue, "stirs up the spirit" of the new foreign king, Cyrus, so he will help the Israelites. Thus, Cyrus becomes YHWH's messiah (Isaiah 45) and YHWH's prophet urges the Israelites returning from exile to follow him. The clashing portrayals of these two foreign emperors, one a mortal enemy, the other an anointed deliverer, are formed by the wildly different ways that Israel's deity works on them.

3 A Divine Life Cycle

The plot of the Hebrew Bible moves in an uneven but determined manner from a deity who is active and present in the world to a silent and distant figure. The former intervenes through both speech and action in an effort to shape human events in the direction he wishes them to go, while the latter is restricted to working through intermediaries or as an internal influence on human beings. At least twice in that long story the deity who has retreated to an existence removed from human action, at the end of Genesis and at the end of the Pentateuch in Deuteronomy, reemerges in a more vigorous form, in Exodus and Joshua respectively, to provide direct assistance to the people of Israel as a divine warrior. As the story of the nation of Israel continued, however, the divine character retreated once again, behind a growing edifice of mediating persons, objects, and activities. While the Hebrew Bible contains an unparalleled quantity of description of divine behavior and speech, its lack of physical description of the deity is remarkable. This may seem a necessary result of the famous command near the beginning of the Ten Commandments at Exodus 20:4, forbidding the making of images, but evidence from ancient Israel indicates that such images were part of the material culture. It was not that ancient Israelites had no ideas about the physical appearance of their deity, only that the literature in the Bible tends not to contain such descriptions, but they are not completely absent.

A powerful and mysterious divine image appears in Daniel 7. The figure is twice named as "the Ancient of Days," and the poet describes him having hair "like pure wool." This is the only place in the Hebrew Bible that provides a direct physical description of Israel's God. It is much more common for the divine appearance to be carefully guarded, as in Ezekiel's "appearance of the likeness of the glory of God." The question this one description raises is how Israel's God became white-haired and old. Jason Bembry has analyzed this question thoroughly, including a discussion of developments of divine characters in Mesopotamian, Levantine, and Hellenistic cultures. The comparisons to Canaanite religion are especially important because the chief God of Canaan, El, is usually portrayed as old, and ancient Israel seems to have had no difficulty equating its God with this figure. At the same time, El had a young and vigorous son named Baal who inherited El's power and is considered throughout the Hebrew Bible to be a forbidden rival of Israel's deity. In the earlier portions of the biblical plot there are no specific physical descriptions, but Israel's God is an active builder and warrior, seemingly a young and vigorous deity. The combination of this inferred youth and the image in Daniel 7 creates a perception that this God has aged.[38] The aging of a deity presents the possibility that starkly different divine portrayals could become a single figure, fitting the sense of monotheism the Hebrew Bible seeks to achieve. Without the long narrative plot to connect them, a young, vigorous deity and an old, less active one might create a sense of multiple beings. How might the idea of an aging God have developed in ancient Israel and how did it incorporate divergent portrayals?

3.1 YHWH as Israel's Husband

The striking and distinctive move in Israelite tradition was to depict Israel as YHWH's wife. There are places like Hosea 1–3 where human marriage may be more purely a metaphor, something to which the relationship between YHWH and Israel might be compared, but Ezekiel 16 tells an explicit story in which YHWH discovers Israel as an abandoned child, waits for her to grow up, and marries her. Telling a story of YHWH marrying Israel and connecting that act to Israel's experience in the wilderness during the exodus and its early growth as a nation in Canaan gave the event a before and after. The before-marriage, marriage, and after-marriage sequence of stages gave Israel's deity the beginnings of a life cycle and made that deity look something like a human. The familial metaphors are mixed in the Hebrew Bible, of course, because YHWH can also look like the father of Israel, but there is still a sense of progress. In places like Jeremiah 2, the political entity called Israel seems to be YHWH's wife, while the Israelite people are the children of these two parents. In all these varied images, Israel's God is connected to a human life cycle, which includes aging.

The confusing mixture of divine metaphors and images takes us back to the discussion of YHWII's relationship to El and Baal, which appeared in Section 1 of this Element. Jason Bembry has asserted that "As older mythic notions were recycled into Israel's present during the postexilic period, refractions of older portrayals, long eschewed by the biblical tradents because of their association with heterodox religious expressions, were deemed admissible in their depictions of [YHWH]."[39] This movement included mixtures of two deities who were father and son. Julia O'Brien has produced a careful examination of the

---

[38] See the discussion in Jason Bembry, *Yahweh's Coming of Age* (Winona Lake, IN: Eisenbrauns, 2011), 91–150.

[39] Ibid., 120.

variety of metaphors prominent in the prophetic literature of the Hebrew Bible: husband, father, warrior, and king. These images of deity are found commonly in the cultures around ancient Israel, so they are not surprising.[40] The Element that is slightly different in the Hebrew Bible is the notion of YHWH as the husband of Israel, a nation or group of people.

For YHWH to be married to Israel may or may not have required him to be unattached to any goddess. Nevertheless, many biblical texts expend considerable effort on this detachment. Evidence outside the Bible from multiple places pair YHWH with a goddess named Asherah.[41] This is another feature of YHWH's identity that overlaps with or displaces the Canaanite god El, to whom Asherah/Athirat was married. The Canaanite god and goddess produced a large number of children together. Inside the Bible, Asherah appears occasionally, but instead of being YHWH's wife she is a foreign deity represented by trees or wooden poles, which some Israelites are condemned for worshipping.[42] Susan Ackerman has argued that Asherah has her own identity and function as the goddess of spinning and weaving. The biblical connection to this role is in places like 2 Kings 23:7, which describes king Josiah destroying a structure within the Jerusalem temple where women were weaving clothes for Asherah. A safer description appears in the description of an ideal woman in Proverbs 31, in which spinning and weaving play significant roles. The humanizing of this goddess figure and avoidance of any names removes the threat of a competing deity or a divine consort.[43] While this anti-Asherah movement may be a late development, part of the recovery from the disasters of the eighth through sixth centuries, it is projected into the distant past. Judges 3:7 includes worship of Asherah as one of the causes for the difficulty Israelites had fully occupying the land upon their arrival from Egypt. When Elijah faces off with the 450 prophets of Baal on Mount Carmel, 1 Kings 18:19 acknowledges the presence of 400 of Asherah, though they become invisible as the story continues. Most interesting is their absence from the description of the subsequent slaughter of the prophets of Baal in the Wadi Kishon in 18:40. Were they taken by the prophets of YHWH, rather than killed, implying a union between YHWH and Ashera?

---

[40] Julia O'Brien, *Challenging Prophetic Metaphor: Theology and Ideology in the Prophets* (Louisville, KY: Westminster John Knox, 2008), 63–124.

[41] References to Asherah inside and outside the Bible are not consistent. They can refer to the goddess herself, or to a cultic object. In the Bible, the relationship between Asherah and a similar figure named Astarte is not always clear. The biblical writers are polemicizing against this alternative pantheon, not trying to give readers a precise description of it. On these difficulties, see Sung Jin Park, "The Cultic Identity of Asherah in Deuteronomistic Ideology of Israel," *Zeitschrift für die Alttestamentliche Wissenschaft* 123 (2011), 553–564.

[42] See the discussion in Stavrakopoulou, *God: An Anatomy*, 149–152.

[43] See Susan Ackerman, *Gods, Goddesses, and the Women Who Serve Them* (Grand Rapids, MI: Eerdmans, 2022), 30–38.

The prophets of the eighth through the sixth centuries were also vehemently opposed to the worship of other gods, but their focus is on Baal and they do not mention Asherah by name. This is one example of how the biblical story accomplishes what Francesca Stavrakopoulou calls a "pantheon reduction," and this makes space for a diverse sense of monotheism. In her words, "In the eyes of the biblical writers, God's traditional wife, Asherah, might have been cast aside, but he retained his position as a divine husband, and wedded himself to his worshippers."[44] The efforts to erase Asherah coincide with the marriage of YHWH to Israel, whether or not it is a necessary precondition.

Discussion of the idea of YHWH marrying Israel demands acknowledgment of the enormous moral problems created by the use of this idea, particularly in the prophetic literature. The terrible dilemma posed by this literature was largely ignored until the emergence of feminist and womanist reading of the Hebrew Bible. It found early expression in the work of Renita Weems in *Battered Love: Marriage, Sex, and Love in the Hebrew Prophets*. A collective human wife for YHWH, living in the human world, was subject to the dangers of that world, yet being the wife of a powerful deity would seem to offer protection from those dangers. The way around those contradictions was to make YHWH, the husband, the source of that danger and the potential protection of it. The result of this choice seems to have generated enormous rhetorical power. As Weems noted, Hosea "used the imagery of sex, romance, and violence to appeal to his audience's inherited cultural values, exploit their greatest fears, and evoke their most sacred traditions."[45] The other side of this is that one of the images that emerged in the portrait of Israel's deity was an abusive husband. One objection to this observation is that the image is "just a metaphor." Gerlinde Baumann has examined the operation of metaphors, applied specifically to the marriage metaphor in the Hebrew Bible, placing essential emphasis on two-way movement of metaphorical language. Metaphors do not just describe reality but also help to form it. Saying repeatedly that God is like a husband generates the idea that a husband is like God. This both excuses the abusive actions of human men toward their wives as godlike and creates an image of the deity that looks like an abusive husband.[46] The feelings of YHWH toward Israel move back and forth from passionate love to revulsion, with Israel's faithfulness, or lack thereof, always blamed for the ugly turns the relationship takes. The portrayal of a very human relationship

---

[44] Ibid., 162.

[45] Renita J. Weems, *Battered Love: Marriage, Sex, and Violence in the Hebrew Prophets* (Minneapolis, MN: Fortress, 1995), 52.

[46] Gerlinde Baumann, *Love and Violence: Marriage as Metaphor for the Relationship between YHWH and Israel in the Prophetic Books* (Collegeville, MN: Liturgical Press, 2003), 27–37.

involving Israel's deity gave him human characteristics that, over time, would help lead to the overwhelming sense that YHWH has become an elderly man.

3.2 Old Age and Divine Embodiment

One need look no further than the stories in the book of Daniel, the book in which the old, white-haired God appears, to see Israel's God acting old. The Aramaic tales that dominate the first half of the book depict Daniel and his young friends in the midst of various difficulties as they live their lives captive to a foreign empire. The God of Israel saves them, but not through obvious acts of power. Daniel does not use God-given strength to tear apart the lions like Samson. Rather, the lions do not maul Daniel, as the furnace does not burn his friends. This latter tale from Daniel 3 even provides some sense of doubt about the divine ability to rescue the young men, though its meaning is entangled in a web of textual and translational difficulties that date back to ancient times. When Shadrach, Meshach, and Abednego speak to Nebuchadnezzar in 3:17–18, with the threat of execution hanging over them, the Masoretic Text of the Hebrew Bible has them say something like, "If our God whom we serve is able to deliver us from the furnace of blazing fire and out of your hand, O king, let him deliver us. But if not, be it known to you O king, that we will not serve your gods." There are two quite different Greek renderings of this text from the ancient world. The so-called Old Greek text says, "There is a God who is in heaven, our one Lord, who is able to deliver us from the furnace of fire, and out of your hands, O king, he will deliver us. And then it will be clear to you that we will neither serve your idol." Not only does this text remove all doubt about their God's ability and willingness to save them by omitting conditional language, it names the Babylonian deity as an "idol" in much more straightforward language. The Greek translation known as the "Theodotion text" falls somewhere in the middle of these two: "for there is a God whom we serve, able to deliver us from the furnace blazing with fire, and out of your hands, O king he will rescue us. And if not, let it be known to you, O king, ..."[47] The tension and uncertainty of these traditions continues in the additional stories added to the Greek additions of Daniel. The story commonly known as Bel and the Dragon introduces an alternative version of the lion's den tale in which an angel carries

---

[47] The initial translation of the Hebrew text comes from the New Revised Standard Version. The English translations of the two Greek versions come from R. Timothy McLay in the *New English Translation of the Septuagint*. The translation of the Masoretic Text by Louis Hartman raises an additional issue, the very existence of the Israelite God, when the young men say, "If there is a God able to save us, such as our God whom we serve." See Louis F. Harman, C.S.S.R., and Alexander A. Di Lella, O. F. M, *The Book of Daniel: A New Translation with Notes and Commentary* (Garden City, NJ: Doubleday, 1978), 155.

a prophet named Habakkuk by the hair from Judah to Persia with food to care for and protect Daniel, placing two layers of mediation between God and Daniel.[48] The God in these stories is a character at some remove from the action taking place in them.

One of the difficulties created by a deity with a life cycle something like humans is that corporeal depictions might conflict with the story. An embodied deity, whether depicted in a material artifact or described in a written text, is frozen in a certain appearance that might limit the flexibility of when and how the character fits into the plot of a narrative. Benjamin Sommer has presented a careful outline of ways that Israel's God appears in bodily form throughout the Hebrew Bible and has demonstrated the many ways interpreters have tried to avoid the subject of divine embodiment.[49] Sommer's work focuses on the fluidity of the divine body in the Bible. One aspect of this fluidity has to do with identity or divine selfhood. God can take on different, independent identities while maintaining a sense of unity. The second aspect is spatial; God can be present in multiple places at the same time. God can be in an ordinary human form, talking and eating with Abraham at Mamre in Genesis 18, or an ethereal human form standing on a sapphire platform on Mount Sinai, eating and drinking with the Israelite elders in Exodus 24, and can also be a giant fearsome being whose hand can cover Moses in the cleft of a rock because only his back is observable to this one human in Exodus 33. While parts of biblical tradition, those that Sommer labels Priestly and Deuteronomic, move away from this sense of fluidity, the Bible retains the traditions that present a fluid deity.[50] McClellan has also demonstrated, through his use of cognitive approaches, how an agent like the ark of the covenant could be a representation of divine presence without being equated with God. The disappearance of a material object like the ark that could represent divine presence gave way to written texts that could perform a similar function.[51] Again, a connected plot helps assure the sense that these appearances and representations all represent a single divine being.

The meeting between God, accompanied by two angels, and Abraham and Sarah in Genesis 18 is one of only two times in the Hebrew Bible where God appears with an ordinary human body. Esther Hamori has labeled this text along with the divine wrestling match with Jacob in Genesis 32 as the only two

---

[48] For a fuller discussion of how the multiple versions of the book of Daniel create a sense of development in the divine character, see Mark McEntire, *An Apocryphal God: Beyond Divine Maturity* (Minneapolis, MN: Fortress, 2015), 80–86.

[49] Benjamin D. Sommer, *The Bodies of God and the World of Ancient Israel* (New York: Cambridge University Press, 2009), 1–11.

[50] Sommer, *The Bodies of God*, 38–76.

[51] Daniel O. McClellan, *YHWH's Divine Images: A Cognitive Approach* (Atlanta, GA: SBL Press, 2022), 135–155.

examples in the Bible of an *'ish* theophany, a divine appearance in ordinary human form. In Genesis 18 God sits and talks with Abraham while they both eat like human beings, and in Genesis 32 God wrestles Jacob to a draw and must injure Jacob in order to escape his grasp.[52] Elsewhere, God's appearance is either super-sized (Exodus 33 and Isaiah 6) or has some supernatural features (Job 38 and Ezekiel 1). It is not surprising that both of the ordinary human appearances take place early in the biblical plot. The theological movements away from embodiedness, physicality, and direct narrative action all make such depictions fit better earlier in the story. At the same time, the divine life cycle, with the marriage of God to Israel at the center of that life, locates these events prior to the marriage, when Israel's God was younger.

The continuous narrative often labeled the Deuteronomistic History tells the story of Israel from the point where Joshua leads the Israelites into the land of Canaan to the destruction of Jerusalem by the Babylonian army. The divine character in this long series of stories does a fair amount of talking. He speaks to Joshua, Samuel, David, Solomon, and others, but this is mostly disembodied speech. The embodied characters who do show up in these texts are typically divine emissaries. For example, Joshua encounters a mysterious figure called the Commander of the Army of YHWH. Joshua's interaction with this figure indicates that he has a normal human body. He appears nowhere else in the Hebrew Bible, and his response to Joshua is strange and ambiguous. By the end of the little episode in Joshua 5:13–15, however, the encounter reflects the experience of Moses at the burning bush in Exodus 3, with Joshua removing his sandals because he is told he is on holy ground. The story of Gideon in Judges 6:11–27 includes an embodied divine being. When this character acts he is described as "the angel of YHWH," and Gideon's behavior toward him indicates he appears as a normal human figure. When the character speaks, however, the speech is attributed directly to YHWH. Eventually, humans, especially kings, require prophets to mediate communication with God, and these strange, embodied characters are relegated to ancient times.

Divine emissaries or representatives are present throughout the biblical tradition, but their identities and characteristics seem to change over time. As the preceding discussion indicates, the "angel of YHWH" often becomes indistinguishable from the deity himself. In stories like Genesis 16, Exodus 3, and Judges 6, we might even see the angel of YHWH as the leading edge of the divine presence. Later, however, angels took on distinct identities of their own. The only two instances of named angels in the Hebrew Bible are Gabriel and

---

[52] Hamori has also documented this phenomenon in the literature of the cultures surrounding ancient Israel, where it was more common. See *When Gods Were Men: The Embodied God in Biblical and Near Eastern Literature* (Berlin: De Gruyter, 2008), 1–25.

Michael, in some of the stories in Daniel 8–12. One of the frequent features of apocalyptic thought and literature, of which Daniel 7–12 is the clearest example in the Hebrew Bible, is the spatial dualism that divides existence into divine and earthly realms, with a boundary that can only be crossed by special beings like angels. Michael and Gabriel are divine agents who can cross this boundary and help humans. They represent God and do God's work but are not part of the divine presence. A more developed example of an angel as a narrative character is in the book of Tobit, included in all versions of the Old Testament except that of Protestant Christianity.[53] As young Tobias, the hero of the story, prepares for his perilous journey, God sends the angel Raphael to help him (3:17). When Tobias goes out to find a traveling companion, he encounters Raphael in the form of a young man whom he calls Azariah ("the Lord helps"). In these later texts, whose writers likely assume God to be an old man, removed from the human world, there are divine agents who are young and vigorous, whom God can send to help humans who are faithful to God.

The problem of God's body and how Judaism and Christianity have tried to dispose of it is one of the themes of recent work by Francesca Stavrakopoulou in *God: An Anatomy*. The conclusion to her work is "an autopsy," because God's body is dead. Stavrakopoulou attributes the initial movement toward this death of the divine body in Israel to the series of destructive events that rained upon Israel beginning in the eighth century. The displacements caused by the destruction of temples in this sequence of events were a threat to an embodied deity who lived in them.[54] It is difficult to say how the death of God's body is related to the aging process of God described in section 3.2. Is the disappearance of the body a solution to the aging problem, the logical conclusion of which would be death? Does the death of the divine body allow the perpetual life of the deity in a disembodied form?

3.3 Divine Survival

The survival of Israel's God accompanied the survival of Israel and its literature. The survival of this people and their texts involved intense work by scribal communities in many places. The quiet, removed, disembodied God of the scribes became the God expressed in most of the Bible. While a future reinvigoration of God appeared in some literature, this idea remained a minor voice in Judaism and Christianity. Apocalyptic literature presented visions of this reinvigoration as a means of survival in contexts of imperial oppression by

---

[53] The place of Tobit within Second Temple Judaism was assured by the identification of fragments of the story in Aramaic and Hebrew among the Dead Sea Scrolls. See Joseph A. Fitzmyer, *Tobit* (Berlin: De Gruyter, 2003), 10–28.

[54] Stavrakopoulou, *God: An Anatomy*, 416–418.

drawing an alternative world.[55] In this alternative world God's presence could look more like the divine character of old. The story of God and the world seems to come full circle in ancient Jewish literature when 1 Enoch 65–68 presents the great flood of Noah as an event at the end of time.[56] The persistent fascination with apocalyptic literature in Christian tradition will be one of the issues treated in Section 5 of this Element.

4 Defeat, Destruction, and Difficult Choices

The narrative connection of Israel's God to the fate of the nation raised a challenging dilemma when the nation faced existential threats and ultimately collapsed beneath their weight. In parallel events, the neo-Assyrian Empire overwhelmed and destroyed the nation of Israel and its capital Samaria in the late eighth century, and the neo-Babylonian Empire did the same to Judah and its capital in Jerusalem in the early sixth century. The identity of Israel had moved and shifted within the biblical story, and the relationship between these two political entities is difficult to discern, but the biblical story centers its perspective on a nation-state(s) of some kind for about four centuries. Considering the relative brevity of this period, it carries surprising weight as a way of thinking about what ancient Israel was and what its deity could do. The previous section already identified the most direct problem. Israel's deity, like others in the region, had come to dwell in one or more temples in cities like Samaria and Jerusalem. What would it mean for foreign invaders to destroy those cities and temples? What would happen to the deity, especially one who had promised always to protect the city?

At the outset of the discussion of this part of Israel's story, some terminological precision is helpful. It is common to use the phrase "ancient Israelite religion" to speak about the period before the destruction of Jerusalem in 586 BCE. The term does useful work, but whether there was something in that time and place distinguishable within Israelite culture as a religion in the modern sense is problematic. As a general rule, it is best to reserve the term "Judaism" for the time after 586, and especially for the postexilic period the biblical story associates with Ezra. One of the reasons for this distinction is the transnational nature of this developing religious system, along with its growing reliance on written traditions. Use of the term "ancient Israel" can add to the confusion, because in the broader field of history "antiquity" often designates the period up to 500 CE, a full millennium beyond the divide between ancient Israelite

---

[55] See Anathea Portier-Young, *Apocalypse Against Empire: Theologies of Resistance in Early Judaism* (Grand Rapids, MI: Eerdmans, 20011), 44–45.

[56] See the discussion of this phenomenon in George W. E. Nickelsburg, *Jewish Literature between the Bible and the Mishnah*, 2nd ed. (Minneapolis, MN: Fortress, 2005), 248–254.

religion and Judaism. Therefore, it is appropriate to use the term "ancient Judaism" for this period, but that can be another source of confusion. I will try to be precise enough in my own terminology, using "ancient Israelite religion" to name the period before the rebuilding of Jerusalem and its temple (approximately 520 BCE), "Second Temple Judaism" for the period from 520 BCE to the destruction of Herod's temple by the Romans in 70 CE, and "Judaism of late antiquity" for the period from the final destruction of the temple through the first five centuries of the Common Era. Maintaining enough clarity about these chronological boundaries is essential to the subject of this Element because monotheism looks different in various eras, in large part because of the experience of destruction and defeat. Ancient Israel's understanding of God had long fallen into the category of henotheism,[57] the belief that every group has their own God and we worship only ours, but defeat made henotheism untenable. If each nation or people had its own deity, then a nation that defeated Israel must have a more powerful one. Instead, writers of the Hebrew Bible typically portrayed Israel's God helping foreign nations to defeat Israel in order to punish its disobedience. David Carr has described this process in the book of Hosea in some detail. When the book of Hosea puts Israel's God on the side of the Assyrian invaders, that deity even begins to resemble this foreign power. "In this way Hosea did a remarkable thing that would shape the course of subsequent religious history: He described Israel's God, Yahweh, as a (partial) reflection of a world-dominating, subordination-demanding Assyrian emperor, an emperor who would settle for nothing less than absolute allegiance."[58] In Carr's words, trauma "became a god-shredder,"[59] and all of the religious traditions that flowed out of Israel's traditions inherited this impact.

4.1 Dislocating the Deity

The association of Israel's God with Jerusalem dominates the Hebrew Bible, even when Deuteronomy can only use the cryptic "place where I will cause may name to dwell" prior to the narrative arrival of the Israelites in the Promised Land. The parallel association of YHWH with the northern capital, Samaria, has thus far only been found in one inscription of uncertain significance.[60]

---

[57] Henotheism is often understood as a middle ground between monotheism and polytheism and is used interchangeably with the term "monolatry," worship of one god without denying the existence of others.

[58] David M. Carr, *Holy Resilience: The Bible's Traumatic Origins* (New Haven, CT: Yale University Press, 2014), 35.

[59] Ibid., 40.

[60] The inscription from an oasis in the Negev desert called Kuntillet Ajrud refers to "YHWH of Samaria and his Asherah," so it associates Israel's deity with both the capital city of the northern

The Hebrew Bible eventually looks at cultic activity in other places, especially northern sites, as illegitimate. When Jeroboam son of Nebat makes the golden calves and places them in Bethel and Dan, as cultic alternatives to Jerusalem, the book of Kings presents this as an act of rebellion and idolatry, worshipping Israel's deity in the form of images. Too many aspects of the story in 1 Kings 12:25–33 look like the more famous golden-calf story in Exodus 32 for the stories to be unrelated. Contrary to what most Bible readers might assume, the relationship between these stories probably works backward, deliberately placing a condemnation of Jeroboam's perceived rebellion back at Israel's origins in the Mount Sinai narrative. Descriptions of idols and idolatry can be problematic because of polemical uses of the terms. Archaeological remains, and even a text like 1 Kings 12, demonstrate that ancient Israelites included images in their worship of YHWH. Accusations of "idolatry" concerning other deities were sometimes political in nature and may not have been strictly tied to the use of images or the conviction that these foreign gods did not exist at all.[61]

The book of Chronicles tells the same story of the division of the kingship after the death of Solomon but omits the story of Jeroboam's golden calves. Once the kingdoms of Israel and Judah split after the death of Solomon, Chronicles is no longer interested in anything that happens in the northern kingdom. Therefore, the destruction of the northern kingdom by Assyria, described in 2 Kings 17, also receives no acknowledgment in Chronicles. Only the destruction of Jerusalem and its temple matter for this strand of Israelite tradition.

Several important cultic sites other than Jerusalem connect to Israel's God in the Bible. In addition to the roughly equivalent "YHWH in Zion" (Psalm 99:2), he is "God of Bethel" (Genesis 31:13), YHWH the one of Sinai (Judges 5:5), and YHWH in Hebron (2 Samuel 15:7).[62] It was Israel's great reformer kings, like Hezekiah and Josiah, urged on by monotheistic prophets, who destroyed many of these other places of worship in an effort to make Jerusalem the only abode of YHWH. At the same time, tradition sought to push the presence of Jerusalem further back into the plot of the Hebrew Bible. The two most famous

kingdom and a feminine divine consort, who in the Bible is routinely disparaged. See the discussion of this place and the inscription in Theodore J. Lewis, *The Origin and Character of God: Ancient Israelite Religion Through the Lens of Divinity* (Oxford: Oxford University Press, 2021), 235–237.

[61] On the political complexities of accusations of idolatry in ancient Israel and its broader context, see Nathaniel Levtow, *Images of Others: Iconic Politics in Ancient Israel* (Winona Lake, IN: Eisenbrauns, 2008).

[62] For a through list of divine names associated with geographical places for Israel and other West Semitic cultures, in the Bible and in other written texts, see Mark S. Smith, *Where the Gods Are: Spatial Dimensions of Anthropomorphism in the Biblical World* (New Haven, CT: Yale University Press, 2016) 72–77.

efforts to do so relate to traditions found in Genesis. A strange story about
Abram's/Abraham's interaction with a priest named Melchizedeck appears in
Genesis 14:17–24. Melchizedeck is also described as "King of Salem." This is
an uncertain place that only appears one other time in the Hebrew Bible (Psalm
76:2). Subsequent versions of the story, such as those found in the work by the
first-century Jewish historian named Josephus called *Jewish Wars* and the early
Aramaic translation of Genesis called *Targum Onkelos* identify the place as
Jerusalem. Likewise, the ambiguous place called Moriah in Genesis 22, where
Abraham travels to offer his son Isaac as a sacrifice, becomes Jerusalem in
subsequent telling of the story like those in 2 Chronicles 3, Jubilees, and
Josephus's *Antiquities of the Jews*.

What would it mean for these cities and the accompanying temple(s) in which
the deity resided to be destroyed by foreign empires? One possible explanation
was that the gods these empires served were more powerful than Israel's God,
but a thoroughly monotheistic view could not abide such a conclusion. The
other alternative, which becomes prominent throughout the Bible in the books
of Kings and Chronicles and the books named for great prophetic figures like
Isaiah, Jeremiah, Ezekiel, Hosea, and Amos, is that Israel's God took the side of
the enemy in order to punish Israel for its disobedience. Ironically, this disobedience is most often characterized as worship of other gods, an act these
other nations would have been performing. The destruction of alternative cultic
sites, whether by external forces like Assyria or by internal forces like the
reform movements of Hezekiah and Josiah, became works of purification.
Traditions that took this perspective in relation to Jerusalem itself typically
looked forward to the survival of a pure remnant and the restoration of the
nation in the future.

Throughout the narratives in the books that report the work of Israel/Judah's
monarchs, Kings and Chronicles, the evaluations of kings focus primarily on
their faithfulness to Israel's God. David becomes the measure of such faithfulness, so that a good king like Asa who reigned over Judah for forty-one years
"did what was right in the sight of YHWH, as his father David had done"
(1 Kings 15:11). On the other hand, Ahab could function as a negative model, so
that Ahaziah, who reigned over Judah in Jerusalem for just one year, "walked in
the way of the house of Ahab, doing what was evil in the sight of YHWH"
(2 Kings 8:27). The idea that Israel's deity had abandoned Jerusalem and joined
their enemies to fight against them was echoed six centuries later by Josephus,
in the wake of the final temple destruction in 70 CE. In *The Jewish War*,
Josephus connected the two defeats explicitly: "The same wonderful sign you
had also experienced formerly, when the forementioned king of Babylon made
war against us, and when he took the city and burnt the temple; . . . Wherefore

I cannot but suppose that God has fled out of his sanctuary, and stands on the side of those against whom you fight."[63] This ideology meant that Israel's God could never lose a battle. Whichever side won, that was the side he had fought for, which was a flexibility that made monotheism function more easily.

The loss of the Jerusalem temple and the experience of captivity in Babylon form a likely matrix for the generation of the kinds of literary works we now know as the books of the Hebrew Bible. The coalescing of older traditions, both written and oral, into large collections allowed for textualized practices that could replace those lost because of destruction and displacement. Reading descriptions of sacrificial rituals in Leviticus, for example, could take the place of the performance of the rituals, if they were no longer possible. Reading the "Songs of Ascents" in Psalms 120–134 could replace the pilgrimage experience of walking up to the temple in Jerusalem. Written texts formed a portable center for those with no access to the temple in Jerusalem, even after it was rebuilt. The multiple ways of considering the story of Israel's deity beyond destruction and dispersion create difficulties for the presentation of this deity. The two closely related movements described in previous sections, away from embodiment and away from direct action as a narrative character, may have provided greater flexibility for these diverse presentations.

The book of Ezra narrates the return of some of the Judahites from Babylon to rebuild Jerusalem. Ezra 3 describes these people arriving in an empty, destroyed Jerusalem that had been purified by destruction and was now ready for rebuilding. The first thing these people do is set up the altar in order to begin offering sacrifices to their God. The book called Ezra-Nehemiah sought to recenter Israel's tradition and the emerging religious system now called Judaism in Jerusalem. It did this by making the experience of exile and return normative, and by treating the worship of Israel's God, YHWH, in Jerusalem as the only possibility for faithfully continuing the traditions of ancient Israel. The reality outside of this part of the Bible was that most people who would have identified themselves with those traditions were living in other places.

4.2 God of Diaspora

The scattering of the people of Israel and Judah in the eighth through fifth centuries created an ongoing challenge for a monotheism that was emerging, promoted by certain figures in the Hebrew Bible, such as the prophets. The grand visions of Ezekiel attempted to address this difficulty. In Ezekiel 1 the prophet

---

[63] This quotation is from the English translation of William Whiston (*The Jewish War* 5:412). See the discussion of these events and reactions to them in Michael L. Satlow, *How the Bible Became Holy* (New Haven, CT: Yale University Press, 2014), 258–261.

reports seeing the great divine chariot in Babylon, while among the exiled people of Judah. The similar vision in Ezekiel 8–10 portrays the same divine presence lifting itself up out of the temple in Jerusalem and flying away to the east, where the exiled citizens of Judah resided. Within the massive vision of a new Jerusalem and a new temple in Ezekiel 40–48, the divine chariot returns to Jerusalem and lowers itself back into the new temple. This final vision may have been helpful and important to those who would return and restore Jerusalem in the late sixth and early fifth centuries, but what did it mean for those who remained in Babylon? Could Israel's God be in many places? Different voices within the Bible offer different ways of answering these questions.

The notion that Israel's deity could be a presence with displaced people was a poor fit with corporeality. Later, the rebuilt temple needed a sense of identity and purpose. If God was in so many places, it was hardly a divine abode anymore. Francesca Stavrakopoulou has pointed toward a possible solution to this dilemma that involved not just the disembodiment of God, but also a more thorough divine transcendence. "The temple would no longer be the dwelling place of God, but an earthly reflection of his far-off heavenly home."[64] Disembodiment and withdrawal from earthly action operate together to reconfigure these issues. The next section will address the nature of this separation between heaven and earth more fully.

The repeated experience of losing the temple in Jerusalem had a profound impact on Judaism. The first loss in 586 BCE not only dislodged YHWH from the house Solomon built for him, it also required a reimagining of the divine presence in other places in the diaspora. When people no longer had access to the divine dwelling in Jerusalem and the rituals that could be performed there, something had to take its place as the focal point of religious experience. One possibility would be to build another temple in another place. The religious ideology of the Hebrew Bible would seem to make this impossible, and for a long time reality seemed to match this assumption. Since the early nineteenth century, archaeologists have been aware of the site on the Nile Delta in Egypt known as Elephantine, but it was not until the 1960s that significant awareness of a Jewish community in this place during the fifth and fourth centuries BCE developed. Only during the first two decades of the twentieth century did a complete enough picture of this community emerge that their temple of YHWH became a prominent subject of study.

The idea that a group of people from Judah fled from the Babylonian invasion, became part of what had been a primarily military community on the Nile Delta, and built a temple there presents a challenge to the dominant

---

[64] Stavrakopoulou, *God: An Anatomy*, 418.

understanding of the Jerusalem temple and its place within ancient Judaism. At very close to the same time that the groups lead by Zerubbabel, Ezra, and Nehemiah were rebuilding Jerusalem and its temple, these other migrants[65] were building and using a temple to worship YHWH in Egypt.[66] Two additional surprising features of the life and practices of this community have emerged. First, though it is an argument from silence, it seems significant that no biblical texts have been found among the writings found at this site. Second, documents and archaeological remains exhibit a diverse picture of worship practices that includes other deities. By the traditional definition, this community looks more polytheistic than the community portrayed in Judah within the Hebrew Bible. Gard Granerød has even argued that this evidence might map back onto the religious experience of Judah, indicating a more diverse set of beliefs than indicated by the ideological texts of the Bible.[67]

The books of the Bible were likely written by a relatively small and homo-genous set of people, to promote their own interests. The notion of exile and return, which dominates the tradition in many ways, helps to illustrate this reality in two ways. First, the number of people who were carried off from Judah into captivity in Babylon was relatively small, and many of those chose not to return to Judah after the collapse of Babylon several decades later. Nevertheless, this portrait of postexilic Judah and Jerusalem became the norm. Books like Chronicles and Ezra-Nehemiah portray the land as having been emptied and then refilled by this process. Archaeological evidence, on the other hand, demonstrates that the majority of Judahites were not taken captive, and that the number of returnees was relatively small.[68] Second, the idea of exile and

---

[65] The terms "exile" for a time period and "exiles" for a limited group of people are problematic. The exile in Babylon for much of the sixth century BCE was the experience of a fairly small group of people, who had an outsized impact on the telling of the story of the Restoration in the Hebrew Bible. Jill Middlemas has suggested the helpful term "Templeless Age" to name the experience of a broader group of people, whose common experience was the loss of the physical center of their community and worship practices. See Jill Middlemass, *The Templeless Age: An Introduction to the History, Literature, and Theology of the "Exile"* (Louisville, KY: Westminster John Knox, 2007), 1–27. See especially her discussion of the emerging picture of cultic practices at Elephantine in Egypt (19–21). The broader term "forced migration" has become common to name the experience of displacement in a way that is not as theologically and ideologically loaded as the term "exile."

[66] For a description of the Elephantine settlement and its temple, see Cornelius von Pilgrim, "On the Archeological Background of the Elephantine Papyri in the Light of Recent Fieldwork," in *Elephantine Revisited: New Insights into the Judean Community and Its Neighbors* (University Park, PA: Pennsylvania State University Press, 2022).

[67] See Gard Granerød, *Dimensions of Yahwism in the Persian Period: Studies in the Religion and Society of the Judaean Community at Elephantine* (Berlin: De Gruyter, 2016), 252–258.

[68] For a careful examination of the archaeological evidence, see Israel Finkelstein, *Hasmonean Realities behind Ezra, Nehemiah, and Chronicles: Archaeological and Historical Perspectives* (Atlanta, GA: SBL Press, 2018), 1–50.

return was stamped onto much of the biblical literature, from the expulsion of Adam and Eve from the Garden of Eden, to the departure to Egypt by Abram and Sarai in Genesis 12, to Jacob's escape to Aram and return to Canaan, to the sojourn of the Israelites in Egypt before the return in the exodus. The Israelite people and their ancestors are always leaving and returning. In Ezra 1–6, all who want to be part of the restored community have to accept this story as their own, regardless of whether they were really part of that small group. The combination of growing understanding of the community in Elephantine, archaeological evidence about life in Judah during the Persian Period, and indications of a thriving community of Jews in Babylon after the exile had ended present a diverse and dispersed portrait of Judaism.[69] The dispersed deity this required became increasingly possible through the processes of disembodiment and withdrawal, but the new issue that arose was whether a disembodied God, withdrawn from the arena of human activity, could be a deliverer like Israel's God of ancient times.

4.3 The Future Divine Warrior

The separation of creation into two places like this is one of the hallmarks of apocalyptic thinking and its accompanying literature, which is frequently called "spatial dualism," described in the previous section of this Element. The experience of defeat elicited many responses and had an ongoing effect on the development of traditions related to the Hebrew Bible. Recent directions in understanding these developments have revealed that the boundaries we see now as a result of the formation of canons are anachronistic and distorting when applied to ancient perceptions. The narrative does not stop when we think we see the collection we know as the Bible reach some particular form. Softening these boundaries, if not removing them, may give us a better picture of the ancient context of reading and writing in Judaism. In one important example of this emerging understanding, Molly Zahn asserted, "This reality, demonstrated spectacularly by the Qumran discoveries, has allowed scholars to move beyond the distinctions between scripture and interpretation, and between composition and transmission, which have been mainstays of Western understandings of the Bible (both lay and scholarly) for hundreds of years."[70] The portions of the Bible that are easiest to identify as apocalyptic, like Daniel and Revelation, look

---

[69] For a description of the Jewish community in Babylon, in the city called Al-Yahudu, see Kathleen Abraham, "The Reconstruction of Jewish Communities in the Persian Empire: The Āl-Yahūdo Clay Tablets," in *Light and Shadows: The Story of Iranian Jews*, ed. David Yeroushalmi (Los Angeles, CA: Fowler Museum at UCLA, 2012), 261–264.

[70] Molly M. Zahn, *Genres of Rewriting in Second Temple Judaism* (Cambridge: Cambridge University Press, 2021), 2.

somewhat isolated within the limited collection of the biblical canon, but wider reading of the literature from that era provides a more thorough and vibrant context. The God of Israel's present at this time may have been obscure, but this deity had a vivid future.

The idea of a decisive future battle, fought by divine forces, may be most familiar to many readers from the final book in the New Testament, Revelation, but it is not a new idea there. Images of Israel's God as a warrior in the future are reflections of Israel's past, when the divine warrior helped them escape from Egypt and establish themselves in the Promised Land. Future wars are part of books that appear to be on the edges of the limited collection in the Hebrew Bible, Daniel on the inside and 1 Enoch on the outside. If we see these boundaries more flexibly and recognize that ideas or images that become clear and prominent in other parts of Second Temple Jewish literature may be present in vague and nascent forms in canonical texts, then a wider view becomes necessary. The War Scroll is known only from its recent appearance among the writings known as the Dead Sea Scrolls. There is one fairly complete manuscript and there are a few fragmentary ones, so the extent of its influence is uncertain. It contains the most explicit description of the final battle between what it calls the Sons of Light and the Sons of Darkness, but there is disagreement among interpreters about how to understand the role these ideas played for those who produced and preserved the War Scroll.[71] The book of Daniel is at best ambivalent about the idea of divine warfare. The accounts in the books called 1 and 2 Maccabees are entirely about human battles fought against an oppressive empire, with vague and subtle divine help. Because the Maccabean literature has not turned up within the Dead Sea Scrolls, there are suggestions that this kind of human warfare was not favored by those who gathered and preserved the scrolls.[72] Parts of 1 Enoch present elaborate images of future war, but these are difficult to connect to hopes or plans for an actual war.[73]

The nebulous nature of this future possibility may be the secret to its persistence in such varied forms. For many modern readers of the Bible a future cataclysmic event, understood as the final battle between good and evil, is a literal expectation. Massive sales of Hal Lindsay's *The Late Great Planet Earth* in the 1970s and the *Left Behind* series in the years surrounding the arrival

---

[71] For a more extensive discussion comparing the perspectives of the War Scroll to other writings, see Shaye J. D. Cohen, *From Maccabees to the Mishnah*, 3rd ed. (Louisville, KY: Westminster John Knox, 2014), 97–100.

[72] For an extensive discussion of factors that may have shaped the contents of the Qumran collection, see Michael E. Stone, *Ancient Judaism: New Visions and Views* (Grand Rapids, MI: Eerdmans, 2011), 31–58.

[73] See further discussion of these comparisons in George W. E. Nickelsburg, *Jewish Literature between the Bible and the Mishnah*, 2nd ed. (Minneapolis, MN: Fortress, 2005), 143–147.

of the new millennium testify to the appeal of these ideas. On the other hand, many readers understand these texts very differently and do not place them at the center of their faith. Portraits of a final battle were a symbolic world offering readers in the Roman period hope in the face of persecution, destruction, and desperation.[74] These observations raise important questions about how readers bring the portrayals of the deity of the Bible into their modern experience. To what extent can views of this deity that differ so greatly still be understood as parts of a monotheistic faith?

5 Arriving at the God of Our Present Experience

It is difficult to overstate the difference between the experiences of Abraham and Sarah and those of Ezra and Nehemiah. Monotheism is a process in which human stories and divine stories continue to interact. The ancestral couple meets, dines with, and talks to their deity, and he talks back to them in normal conversation. He also commands one of them to murder their only child, while promising him countless descendants. The later figures, having led the Israelites back to Jerusalem after the exile, pray fervently to their God for guidance and assistance to resolve the difficulties of the returned community, but this deity does not say a word in response. They resort to torturing and banishing other human beings to try to please God. As Jack Miles so elegantly put it, "It makes the Lord seem less like the Jews' creator, liege, father, or king and more like their enfeebled but cherished ward. His may have been the honor, but theirs is the vigor."[75] If the divine voice is present at all late in the plot of the Hebrew Bible, it is within a text, read aloud by Ezra the scribe.

It is difficult to know the contents of the scroll Ezra reads aloud to the people in Nehemiah 8. Readers of the book of Nehemiah might assume it is the entire Torah, but this seems too long and complex to fit the story. Some form of the book of Deuteronomy seems more likely in terms of length and purpose. Regardless of the precise contents, the scroll is the only way YHWH speaks in this part of the story. He has become a deity inside a book. The divine reticence in this later period may be resolved by the reading of a scroll and imagining a divine voice. The book of Deuteronomy and one of its afterlives offer a tantalizing possibility for understanding this process. YHWH tends not to speak directly in the fifth book of the Bible, which is dominated by the voice of Moses, but most often Moses is reporting what YHWH has said to him.[76]

---

[74] Anathea Portier-Young, *Apocalypse Against Empire: Theologies of Resistance in Early Judaism* (Grand Rapids, MI: Eerdmans, 2011), 382–389.

[75] Jack Miles, *God: A Biography* (New York: Vintage Books, 1995), 373.

[76] The small amount of direct divine speech to Moses in the death narrative of Deuteronomy 34 is from another source of the Pentateuch and would have appeared naturally near the end of the

The layers of mediation in Deuteronomy are curious. The voice of YHWH is audible only to Moses, who speaks to the Israelites inside the book. If the scribe must then read the book to an audience, as Ezra may have been doing in Nehemiah 8, there are as many as three layers of mediation between the divine voice and the listener. But why must a written text be further mediated? The text known as the Temple Scroll has appeared so far only among the manuscripts found in the Judean Desert, commonly known as the Dead Sea Scrolls. Therefore, it is typically placed in the group of texts described as "sectarian scrolls," writings unique to the group of people who apparently placed these scrolls in the caves where they were found in the middle of the twentieth century. Much of the Temple Scroll reproduces the legal corpus found in Deuteronomy 12–26, the Deuteronomic Code, with some important changes. Along with some updating of language, there is a striking change in voice. Instead of Moses quoting YHWH, the deity speaks directly to the reader or hearer of the text. The written text has taken the place of Moses as the divine mediator.[77] The idea that a text can be close to divine may be reflected in Nehemiah 8 when Ezra holds the scroll in front of the people, and they apparently bow down to it.[78]

It is difficult to know with certainty how people at different times in ancient Israel experienced God or thought about divine presence, but there are additional traces within the books of the Hebrew Bible. Jeremiah 36 tells a fascinating story about the great prophet, his scribe Baruch son of Neriah, and a variety of political figures, including King Jehoiakim. In the story, YHWH commands Jeremiah to write in a scroll all the words YHWH has spoken to him. What Jeremiah does is dictate these words to Baruch, who writes them down. When King Jehoiakim finally hears about this scroll, he has it read to him and burns it piece by piece as the reader finishes. Jeremiah 36:32 informs readers that Baruch made another copy of the scroll, to which he added additional words. The story creates the idea of at least four layers of scroll development: 1. A prophet speaks words that mediate a divine utterance, 2. the prophet later repeats these words to a scribe who writes them down, 3) the scribe later writes another scroll with words he has added, and 4) a later scribe writes the present scroll that includes the story of all the earlier scroll-making. This idea pushes the phenomenon of divine speech to the prophet back several steps in the process.

---

book of Numbers, but the compiler of the Pentateuch had to extend the life of Moses in order to present all of his speeches in Deuteronomy.

[77] For more explanation of these changes, see Bernard M. Levinson, *A More Perfect Torah: At the Intersection of Philology and Hermeneutics in Deuteronomy and the Temple Scroll* (Winona Lake, IN: Eisenbrauns, 2013), 89–92.

[78] See the discussion of this in Miles, *God: A Biography*, 388–389.

The process is similar to Ezra reading a book of laws that YHWH spoke to Moses years ago. In both cases Israel's deity spoke to important figures in the past, and that speech was transmitted and presented to a later audience through multiple layers of communal work. The distant and disembodied deity that this Element has been describing can appear in complex ways within these expansive and growing literary works.

5.1 The Changing Portrait of God

Earlier portions of this Element have demonstrated literary processes in the Hebrew Bible that moved the reader from an unfamiliar world to a more familiar one. A helpful and entertaining example is the array of changes that take place when the plot of Genesis moves from the primeval world to the world of the Israelite ancestors. Table 2 lists some of those changes.

The combined effect of these changes likely meant that for the earliest readers or hearers of the book of Genesis, characters like the ancestors – Abraham, Sarah, Hagar, Isaac, Rebekkah, Jacob, Rachel, and Leah – were familiar. These readers may not have lived their lives like the ancestors, because they were likely to have been more urban, but they had at least seen people who lived like this. The last item in the list is the most important for this discussion. The dominant character at the middle of the book of Genesis, Jacob, has a variety of encounters with YHWH. The first encounter is inside a dream in Genesis 28 and happens at a very specific place, Bethel. The dream encounter has happened before in Genesis, but with a foreign king, Abimelech of Gerar, in Genesis 26. Abraham's encounter with YHWH in Genesis 15 is mysterious and difficult to describe. Abraham falls into a deep sleep in 15:12, and YHWH speaks to him just after this in v. 13, so he may or may not be dreaming. YHWH has already been speaking to Abraham earlier in this story while

Table 2 Narrative characteristics of Genesis 1–11 and Genesis 12–50.a

Genesis 1–11	Genesis 12–50
Characters live for many hundreds of years	Characters live just over 100 years
Vague geography or none at all	Precise location of events
Undeveloped characters	Highly developed characters
Quick movement through many generations	Careful attention to each generation
Lack of human-to-human dialogue	Lots of interaction between humans
Divine–human speech without introduction	Divine–human speech decreases and requires more specific context

he was awake, so if it is a dream then it is an exception to their usual way of interacting. The movement goes one step further to divine revelation through symbolic dreams in the Joseph narratives of Genesis 37–50. Divine communication through symbolic dreams is a phenomenon the earliest readers of Genesis would have recognized.

Another important place where a progression in divine presence is visible is in the books called Job and Ecclesiastes. These two works have long been classified in biblical scholarship as "wisdom literature." This is a problematic category, and these two books are quite different in form, but they share similar concerns. For the character named Job and the character in Ecclesiastes identified as Qohelet ("the Teacher"), the experience of life is not measuring up to the assumptions of their traditions. Job is a "blameless and upright" man who has been receiving all of the blessings of success that supposedly come as a result of that way of living, but suddenly loses them. Qohelet is a wise person who "taught the people knowledge" and "wrote words of truth plainly" (Ecclesiastes 12:9–10), but by his own admission he can see no logic in the operation of the world. All of his efforts amount to "emptiness,"[79] and a "chasing after wind." While the story of Job is one that does not fit easily in the timeline or geography presented by the primary plot of the Hebrew Bible, Ecclesiastes places its main character in Jerusalem during the monarchy, the central time and place in Israel's story. Job demands an explanation of his fate, and after a long dialogue with his friends he finally receives a divine visit in Job 38. The deity becomes a speaking character and his entrance into the story brings about a resolution, even if it is not fully satisfying. While Qoheleth speaks about the divine character, the human character does not ask for a divine audience, and the book ends with its questions unresolved. There is never any sense in Ecclesiastes that God could appear and speak. He is as distant and silent as in Ezra-Nehemiah.

5.2 Troubles with a Changing God

The idea that "God never changes" is common in many Christian contexts. Those who have read the Hebrew Bible, which forms the basis of the various Old Testaments within Christianity, without this idea as a fixed assumption may wonder how it can survive even a moderately careful reading. The divine character in the Bible is constantly shifting and changing. Soon after creating humans, God regrets the act and decides to annihilate them with a flood

---

[79] The characteristic word of this speaker, *hebel*, has long been translated into English as "vanity," thanks to the ongoing influence of the King James Version. Emptiness or meaningless are probably better renderings in contemporary English.

(Genesis 6:6). While a few English translations use the word "repented" to describe God's action here, most use "regretted" or "was sorry." God initially resists the idea of appointing a king over Israel, then approves the choice of Saul as king, then expresses sorrow over the choice (1 Samuel 8–16). God promises eternal kingship to David and his descendants, then destroys the kingdom of Judah, ending the monarchy (Psalm 89). The most frequently cited text on divine immutability is probably Malachi 3:6, a verse near the end of the final book in every version of the Old Testament. The full verse says, "For I am the LORD, I do not change; and you are the children, you are not finished." In this book where the survival of Israel is in question, this looks like a reaffirmation of YHWH's commitment to their continued existence. Extracting the first half of the verse and making it a defining quality of Israel's deity is a choice that seems to move away from the statement's intent, but it is easy to see how, in a rapidly changing and threatening world, such a statement from God might be appealing. There are two kinds of difficulties with this idea of divine immutability. One is the frequency with which the divine character in the Hebrew Bible changes course within particular stories, as mentioned in chapter 2. The other is the kind of broad, sweeping change in the nature of the divine character that takes place across the full plot of the Hebrew Bible. This Element has demonstrated three of these changes, using texts from the Bible and in the remains of material culture from the places where these texts emerged. First, Israel's God begins the story as an active, speaking character who intervenes in the world on behalf of his people but ends as a withdrawn, silent figure who exerts internal influence on human characters who claim to do his bidding. Second, Israel's God appears to be young and vigorous in early parts of the story and becomes attached to a human life cycle by the use of marriage imagery to describe the relationship between him and Israel. As the story progresses, the deity ages and is eventually described as a white-haired, ancient figure. Third, at various places in the story and in material artifacts, Israel's God once had a body. This body could look like an ordinary human one, or it could be superhuman in some ways. As time went by, however, God became disembodied. All three of these changes contribute to and benefit from a movement toward monotheism, but the persistence of earlier versions of the deity present ongoing difficulties.

Two influential ways of dealing with these apparent changes are "covenant theology" and "dispensationalism." Both systems divide the biblical story and human history into distinct periods and argue that the arrangement between God and humans is different in each period. The most important divide in each is the crucifixion and resurrection of Jesus, which begins the "New Covenant" or the "Dispensation of Grace." The details of both systems can become quite extravagant, but what they attempt to do is separate

God's being, which is immutable, from the way the divine–human relationship functions throughout a preconceived plan that includes different eras. Among the many problems these systems create is the central assertion that the God portrayed in the Bible has replaced Israel with the Christian church as God's human partner in the redemption of the world. The view often called "supersessionism" generates or amplifies a wide variety of anti-Semitic beliefs and behaviors. In this system the God of the Bible is consistent in demanding justice for human disobedience, but Jesus takes the necessary punishment, permitting God to forgive humans. This arrangement allows for a presumed consistency in God's character despite an apparent shift in God's treatment of some humans, the ones who agree to the new arrangement. The cost is the separation this creates between Jews and Christians. The former have been abandoned by their deity, unless they join the latter. This is not a story told in fully developed form in the New Testament, but there are bits and pieces that those who presume the story can put together in order to create a sense of biblical support. Christians who adopt this story are able to claim a monotheism that extends back to the book of Genesis, and they often find the presence of Jesus in the plural divine language of 1:26–27 and YHWH's statement to the snake in 3:15. In its most insidious form, this group sees the Jewish people not just as a group abandoned by God but also as responsible for the killing of God's son.[80]

Despite more than 2000 years of intense development, the singular deity presumed by traditions related to the Hebrew Bible is not a simple, stable entity. For many Christian readers, the divine character in the Hebrew Bible presents an ongoing challenge. Whether this being can be the same as the God whom Jesus calls Father in the Christian New Testament is a controversy that goes back at least to the middle of the second century and the teachings of Marcion, which were declared heretical by church authorities in Rome. Marcion produced his own Bible, which included none of the Old Testament and was limited to parts of the gospel of Luke plus most of the epistles attributed to Paul. The controversy surrounding Marcion and the persistent reading practices among many Christian communities to this day reveal the challenge of incorporating all of this divine characterization into a single figure. Eric Siebert addressed this problem directly in *Disturbing Divine Behavior: Troubling Old Testament Images of God*, a book that created significant controversy when it appeared in 2009. After presenting some of the passages he finds most troubling and introducing some of the groups of people who find them disturbing, Siebert

---

[80] For some of this history, see Karen Armstrong, *Fields of Blood: Religion and the History of Violence* (New York: Knopf, 2015), 211–224, and James Carroll, *Constantine's Sword: The Church and the Jews, a History* (Boston, MA: Houghton Mifflin, 2001), 237–277.

described a common way of dealing with these difficulties: "Holding tightly to clearly defined ideas about the nature of God, they immediately find ways to justify or resolve any theological tension they feel when reading potentially problematic passages."[81] In contrast to this there are many readers who find these images of the divine tremendously difficult. Perhaps the most significant groups are those who have suffered injustice and oppression, with these passages used as motivation or justification. Siebert's response to these problematic passages likely expressed out loud what many have been thinking quietly, that these portraits represent an inaccurate portrait of the Christian God. Siebert distinguishes between a "textual God" and an "actual God," a move that resembles Marcion's editing of the Bible.[82] While Siebert does not remove difficult texts from the Bible, rather insisting they be confronted, removing them from the portrait of an "actual God" that exists outside of the text has similar effects.

Another approach would be to accept that no text can offer an accurate account of a being outside of that text. Disputes about the nature of Israel's God appear within the Hebrew Bible itself. A famous one is present in texts near to one another in Exodus 33. Verse 11 says, "Thus YHWH spoke to Moses face to face, as one speaks to a companion," while in verse 20 YHWH says to Moses, "You can not see my face, for none can see me and live." There are many other texts taking either side of this debate about whether a human can see God. When modern worshippers speak of seeing or hearing God they mean many different things. Debates about the nature of religious experience continue, and the Bible cannot provide definitive answers. The Bible also offers many different perspectives on the God's relationship to violence and can host a serious debate on the issue, but it does not settle the question of whether God continues to commit acts of violence. Claims about such acts differ widely among those who worship the God they relate to the Bible.

5.3 Concluding Observations

The discussion in this Element has returned frequently to the observation that the long narrative portrayal of God in the Bible demonstrates three processes that contribute to the possibility of monotheism. One of these is the disembodiment of God. Movement away from the depiction of God as a being with a physical body limits the ways in which these physical representations might differ and create difficulties for thinking about a singular being. Second, the

---

[81] Eric A. Siebert, *Disturbing Divine Behavior: Troubling Old Testament Images of God* (Minneapolis, MN: Fortress, 2009), 51.

[82] See Siebert's presentation of this process. Ibid., 170–173.

Hebrew Bible portrays an aging deity. The powerful divine warrior who rescues Israel from bondage and takes Israel as his wife eventually becomes the "Ancient of Days." Even though the presentation of God moves away from embodiment, the fragments of physical imagery that remain are elderly, helping to render God's physicality less important. Finally, the deity becomes more silent and removed as the plot of the Bible progresses. The active character who speaks to humans and intervenes in world affairs becomes a being to whom humans pray and who acts internally and invisibly to influence the behavior of humans. Depictions that might cause difficulty for monotheistic belief become part of the early development of a singular character who only looks different at different stages of the story. The Hebrew Bible as a whole does not present a rigorous monotheism, but its literary portrayal of Israel's deity moves in that direction and provides possibilities for continued movement.

References

Abraham, Kathleen. "The Reconstruction of Jewish Communities in the Persian Empire: The Āl- Yahūdo Clay Tablets." In *Light and Shadows: The Story of Iranian Jews*, ed. David Yeroushalmi, 261–264. Los Angeles, CA: Fowler Museum at UCLA, 2012.

Ackerman, Susan. *Gods, Goddesses, and the Women Who Serve Them*. Grand Rapids, MI: Eerdmans, 2022.

Armstrong, Karen. *Fields of Blood: Religion and the History of Violence*. New York: Knopf, 2015.

Baumann, Gerlinde. *Love and Violence: Marriage as Metaphor for the Relationship between YHWH and Israel in the Prophetic Books*. Collegeville, MN: Liturgical Press, 2003.

Bembry, Jason. *Yahweh's Coming of Age*. Winona Lake, IN: Eisenbrauns, 2011.

Carr, David M. *Holy Resilience: The Bible's Traumatic Origins*. New Haven, CT: Yale University Press, 2014.

Carroll, James. *Constantine's Sword: The Church and the Jews, a History*. Boston, MA: Houghton Mifflin, 2001.

Cline, Eric H. *1177 B. C.: The Year Civilization Collapsed*. Princeton, NJ: Princeton University Press, 2014.

Cohen, Shaye J. D. *From Maccabees to the Mishnah*, 3rd ed. Louisville, KY: Westminster John Knox, 2014.

Coogan, Michael D. and Mark S. Smith, eds. *Stories from Ancient Canaan*, 2nd ed. Louisville, KY: Westminster John Knox, 2012.

Finkelstein, Israel. *Hasmonean Realities behind Ezra, Nehemiah, and Chronicles: Archaeological and Historical Perspectives*. Atlanta, GA: SBL Press, 2018.

Fitzmyer, Joseph A. *Tobit*. Berlin: De Gruyter, 2003.

Fleming, Daniel E. *The Legacy of Israel in Judah's Bible: History, Politics, and the Reinscribing of Tradition*. Cambridge: Cambridge University Press, 2012.

Flood, Gavin. *Hindu Monotheism*. Cambridge: Cambridge University Press, 2020.

Friedman, Richard Elliott. *The Disappearance of God: A Divine Mystery*. Boston, MA: Little, Brown, 1995.

Granerød, Gard. *Dimensions of Yahwism in the Persian Period: Studies in the Religion and Society of the Judaean Community at Elephantine*. Berlin: De Gruyter, 2016.

Greenstein, Edward L. *Job: A New Translation*. New Haven, CT: Yale University Press, 2019.

Guttiérrez, Gustavo. *On Job: God-Talk and the Suffering of the Innocent*. Maryknoll, NY: Orbis, 1987.

Hamori, Esther. *When Gods Were Men: The Embodied God in Biblical and Near Eastern Literature*. Berlin: De Gruyter, 2008.

Harman, Louis F. C. S. S. R. and Alexander A. Di Lella, O. F. M. *The Book of Daniel: A New Translation with Notes and Commentary*. Garden City, NJ: Doubleday, 1978.

Humphreys, W. Lee. *The Character of God in the Book of Genesis*. Louisville, KY: Westminster John Knox, 2001.

Kim, Yung Suk. *Monotheism, Biblical Traditions, and Race Relations*. Cambridge: Cambridge University Press, 2022.

Levenson, Jon D. *Sinai and Zion: An Entry into the Jewish Bible*. San Francisco, CA: Harper & Row, 1985.

Levinson, Bernard M. *A More Perfect Torah: At the Intersection of Philology and Hermeneutics in Deuteronomy and the Temple Scroll*. Winona Lake, IN: Eisenbrauns, 2013.

Levtow, Nathaniel. *Images of Others: Iconic Politics in Ancient Israel*. Winona Lake, IN: Eisenbrauns, 2008.

Lewis, Theodore J. *The Origin and Character of God: Ancient Israelite Religion through the Lens of Divinity*. Oxford: Oxford University Press, 2021.

McClellan, Daniel O. *YHWH's Divine Images: A Cognitive Approach*. Atlanta, GA: SBL Press, 2022.

McEntire, Mark. *An Apocryphal God: Beyond Divine Maturity*. Minneapolis, MN: Fortress, 2015.

Portraits of a Mature God: Choices in Old Testament Theology. Minneapolis, MN: Fortress, 2013.

Middlemass, Jill. *The Templeless Age: An Introduction to the History, Literature, and Theology of the "Exile."* Louisville, KY: Westminster John Knox, 2007.

Miles, Jack. *God: A Biography*. New York: Vintage, 1995.

Mobley, Gregory. *The Return of the Chaos Monsters*. Grand Rapids, MI: Eerdmans, 2012.

Ngwa, Kenneth N. *Let My People Live: An Africana Reading of Exodus*. Louisville, KY: Westminster John Knox, 2022.

Nickelsburg, George W. E. *Jewish Literature between the Bible and the Mishnah*, 2nd ed. Minneapolis, MN: Fortress, 2005.

O'Brien, Julia. *Challenging Prophetic Metaphor: Theology and Ideology in the Prophets*. Louisville, KY: Westminster John Knox, 2008.

Park, Sung Jin. "The Cultic Identity of Asherah in Deuteronomistic Ideology of Israel." *Zeitschrift für die alttestamentliche Wissenschaft* 123 (2011), pp. 553–564.

von Pilgrim, Cornelius. "On the Archaeological Background of the Elephantine Papyri in the Light of Recent Fieldwork." In *Elephantine Revisited: New Insights into the Judean Community and Its Neighbors*, ed. Margaretha Folmer, 1–16. University Park, PA: Pennsylvania State University Press, 2022.

Portier-Young, Anathea. *Apocalypse Against Empire: Theologies of Resistance in Early Judaism*. Grand Rapids, MI: Eerdmans, 2011.

Satlow, Michael L. *How the Bible Became Holy*. New Haven, CT: Yale University Press, 2014.

Schäfer, Peter. *Two Gods in Heaven: Jewish Concepts of God in Antiquity*. Trans. Allison Brown. Princeton, NJ: Princeton University Press, 2020.

Seow, C. L. *Job 1–21: Interpretation and Commentary*. Grand Rapids, MI: Eerdmans, 2013.

Siebert, Eric A. *Disturbing Divine Behavior: Troubling Old Testament Images of God*. Minneapolis, MN: Fortress, 2009.

Smith, Mark S. *The Origins of Biblical Monotheism: Israel's Polytheistic Background and the Ugaritic Texts*. Oxford: Oxford University Press, 2001.
The Priestly Vision of Genesis 1. Minneapolis, MN: Fortress, 2010.
Where the Gods Are: Spatial Dimensions of Anthropomorphism in the Biblical World. New Haven, CT: Yale University Press, 2016.

Sommer, Benjamin D. *The Bodies of God and the World of Ancient Israel*. New York: Cambridge University Press, 2009.

Stavrakopoulou, Francesca. *God: An Anatomy*. New York: Knopf, 2022.

Stone, Michael E. *Ancient Judaism: New Visions and Views*. Grand Rapids, MI: Eerdmans, 2011.

Strollo, Megan Fullerton. *Theologies of Human Agency: Counterbalancing Divine In/Activity in the Megilloth*. New York: Lexington Books, 2022.

VanderKam, James C. *Jubilees*. Minneapolis, MN: Fortress, 2020.

Weems, Renita J. *Battered Love: Marriage, Sex, and Violence in the Hebrew Prophets*. Minneapolis, MN: Fortress, 1995.

Zahn, Molly M. *Genres of Rewriting in Second Temple Judaism*. Cambridge: Cambridge University Press, 2021.

Acknowledgments

Thank you first to Paul K. Moser and Chad Meister for conceiving this Element series and for inviting my contribution to it in this volume. The privilege of writing something that falls in between the length of a standard journal article and a monograph opens up great possibilities. I am also grateful to the editorial staff at Cambridge University Press for their work. My ongoing research feedback group among my colleagues at Belmont University consists of Amanda Miller, Ann Coble, Beth Ritter-Conn, and Wongi Park. They read the initial proposal and some section drafts and offered specific feedback, and their steady encouragement helps sustain my work. Joseph Ryan Kelly also read drafts of some sections and provided helpful suggestions. Thank you to all of these people and many others who continue to make my research and writing possible.

Cambridge Elements ≡

Religion and Monotheism

Paul K. Moser

Loyola University Chicago

Paul K. Moser is Professor of Philosophy at Loyola University Chicago. He is the author of *Paul's Gospel of Divine Self-Sacrifice*; *The Divine Goodness of Jesus*; *Divine Guidance*; *Understanding Religious Experience*; *The God Relationship*; *The Elusive God* (winner of national book award from the Jesuit Honor Society); *The Evidence for God*; *The Severity of God*; *Knowledge and Evidence* (all Cambridge University Press); and *Philosophy after Objectivity* (Oxford University Press); coauthor of *Theory of Knowledge* (Oxford University Press); editor of *Jesus and Philosophy* (Cambridge University Press) and *The Oxford Handbook of Epistemology* (Oxford University Press); and coeditor of *The Wisdom of the Christian Faith* (Cambridge University Press). He is the coeditor with Chad Meister of the book series *Cambridge Studies in Religion, Philosophy, and Society.*

Chad Meister

Affiliate Scholar, Ansari Institute for Global Engagement with Religion, University of Notre Dame

Chad Meister is Affiliate Scholar at the Ansari Institute for Global Engagement with Religion at the University of Notre Dame. His authored and coauthored books include *Evil: A Guide for the Perplexed* (Bloomsbury Academic, 2nd edition); *Introducing Philosophy of Religion* (Routledge); *Introducing Christian Thought* (Routledge, 2nd edition); and *Contemporary Philosophical Theology* (Routledge). He has edited or coedited the following: *The Oxford Handbook of Religious Diversity* (Oxford University Press); *Debating Christian Theism* (Oxford University Press); with Paul Moser, *The Cambridge Companion to the Problem of Evil* (Cambridge University Press); and with Charles Taliaferro, *The History of Evil* (Routledge, in six volumes). He is the coeditor with Paul Moser of the book series *Cambridge Studies in Religion, Philosophy, and Society.*

About the Series

This Cambridge Element series publishes original concise volumes on monotheism and its significance. Monotheism has occupied inquirers since the time of the Biblical patriarch, and it continues to attract interdisciplinary academic work today. Engaging, current, and concise, the Elements benefit teachers, researchers, and advanced students in religious studies, Biblical studies, theology, philosophy of religion, and related fields.

Cambridge Elements ⁼

Religion and Monotheism

Printed in the United States
by Baker & Taylor Publisher Services